Eyewitn

Eyewitness at Wounded Knee

Richard E. Jensen, R. Eli Paul, and John E. Carter

University of Nebraska Press: Lincoln & London

for Printed Library Materials, ANZI Z39.48- 1984 ¶ Library of Congress Cataloging

in Publication Data ¶ Jensen, Richard E. ¶ Eyewitness at Wounded Knee / Richard

E. Jensen, R. Eli Paul, and John E. Carter ¶ p. cm. — (Great plains photography

series) ¶ Includes bibliographical references and index ¶ ISBN 0-8032-1409-X (alkaline

paper) ¶ 1. Wounded Knee Creek, Battle of, 1890. 2. Wounded Knee Creek, Battle

of, 1890 — Pictorial works. 3. Dakota Indians — Wars, 1890-1891. 4. Dakota

Indians — Wars, 1890-1891 — Pictorial works. I. Paul, R. Eli, 1954-. II. Carter,

John, 1950-. III. Title. IV. Series ¶ E83.89. J461991 973.8'6—dc20 90-48631 CIP

¶ This volume in the Great Plains Photography Series is made possible by a grant from

the University of Nebraska Foundation to extend the work of the University beyond its

campuses ¶ Typeset in the Linotype Corporation's version of Mr. Eric Gill's Joanna.

Designed by R. Eckersley at the University of Nebraska Press. Second printing, 1992.

Contents

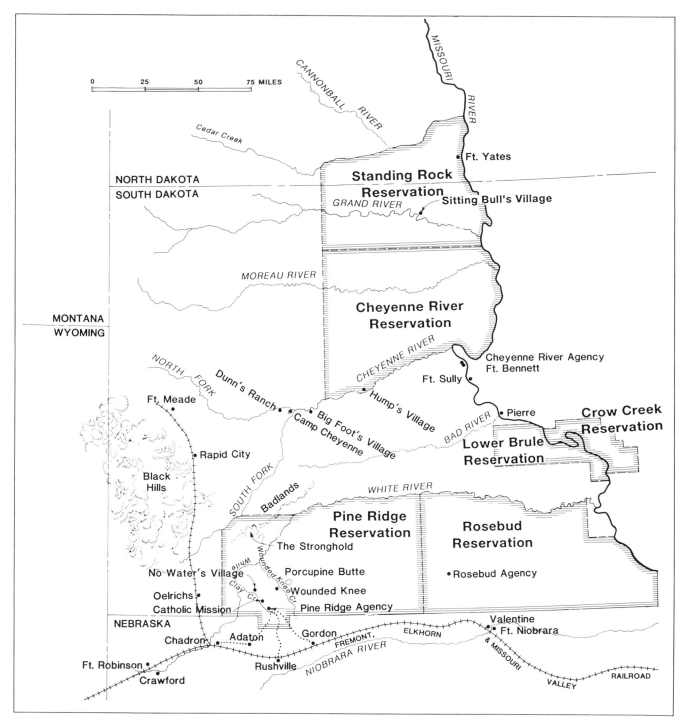

Sioux Reservations, 1890

Foreword

On the morning of December 29, 1890, near a creek named Wounded Knee, the Seventh Cavalry of the United States Army attempted to disarm a Sioux Indian village. Its residents were the followers of Big Foot and of the recently slain Sitting Bull. They had escaped arrest once already and had fled from the north to the protection of their Pine Ridge kinsmen, until intercepted the day before by the soldiers and escorted to a campsite along the Wounded Knee. On that Monday morning, in a charged atmosphere of mutual distrust and misunderstanding, it took only the firing of one Indian gun to set off the wholesale killing of Indian men, women, and children and of soldiers. Wounded Knee is a major symbol of the clash of cultures, of failed government Indian policy, and of the end of the frontier. It has also been a fertile subject for generations of scholars, novelists, and poets. ¶ I grew up near the battlefield and became acquainted with many descendants of the battle's participants. I soon realized the continuing emotional impact of the Ghost Dance era both on the Indians who lived on the Pine Ridge Reservation and on the tourists who flocked there each summer to visit the historic site. No one who was interested in western history could have been unaware of or unaffected by the often-reproduced images of Wounded Knee's aftermath—the macabre and gruesome portrait of Big Foot's twisted corpse, or the still, frozen bodies stacked on a wagon and in the burial trench. Those photographs brought home the reality of plains warfare. ¶ In 1970, while researching a master's thesis on Lakota material culture, I learned that there were many unpublished or rarely used photographs relating to Wounded Knee. A decade ago I decided a photographic history of the tragedy would be an important future research project. The perfect opportunity came along when the Nebraska State Historical Society purchased a magnificent and apparently unique souvenir album made shortly after the 1890–91 Sioux campaign. It may have been assembled by one of the photographers who were there, although this remains unknown. Many of the 101 vintage albumen photographs were unique, and all had captions that helped to explain the images as well as those held elsewhere. Together with the already significant photographic holdings of the Society, they formed a major collection. By happy coincidence, the Society had just created a Division of Research to coordinate and execute institutional research projects. This book is the result of the labors of three Society scholars over two years. (Photographs from the album are designated in "Photograph Repositories," as W938-119.) ¶ I have followed their progress with great interest, both as a supervisor and as a historian. Initial plans to publish the album itself were cast aside soon after the research was begun. Our anonymous album maker used no discernible criteria in selecting the photographs or determining their order, and many of the captions proved to be incorrect. All three researchers came to realize that the photographs surviving from the Wounded Knee episode were not the planned documentation of a historical event. An appropriate context had to be provided. ¶ Although photographs have been used extensively in previous works on Wounded Knee, secondary sources have made few references to the photographers themselves. The researchers had to sort through a mass of primary sources in order to carry out the basic documentation of the photographs. This required gathering all known eyewitness accounts and photographs in the Society's collections, as well as those from other repositories. Primary sources cited in the authors' text and the institutions acknowledged in the appendix reflect these efforts. ¶ Richard Jensen's chapter "Another Look at Wounded Knee," provides a fresh look at the Indian side of Wounded Knee by reexamining the original ethnohistorical sources. Jensen documents misinterpretations and factual errors appearing in earlier scholarship, errors that have been repeated to form a significant though inaccurate part of the existing interpretive record. The chapter is based upon Jensen's clear understanding of the political and economic quagmire in which the Sioux found themselves after 1877, a desperate time of defiance by a people who had at long last come to understand what the future had in store for them. ¶ R. Eli Paul's chapter, "Your Country Is Surrounded," reinterprets the army's role in Wounded Knee. It has been widely held that the Sioux campaign of 1890–91 was the last campaign of the Indian Wars, Wounded Knee was the last battle, and, symbolically, the Seventh Cavalry had been selected by fate or design to settle old scores with the Sioux. However, that interpretation is difficult to sustain, since other Indian battles occurred a decade or more later in Oklahoma, Wyoming, Nevada, and California. Wounded Knee can just as easily be seen as the beginning of a new era in which technology—the telegraph, the telephone, and the railroad—transformed the Wild West into the Old West. ¶ John Carter's chapter, "Making Pictures for a News-Hungry Nation," deals with a relatively unstudied topic—the photographers and (to a lesser extent) the reporters, all of whom were looking for something to sell. The Ghost Dance troubles offered an important opportunity for local newsmen to reach a national audience; only three reporters had the foresight or luck to actually be at the Battle of Wounded Knee, and all three were from nearby Nebraska. The photographers, none of whom were at the actual battle, capitalized on the national attention and produced hundreds of images, both good and bad. The Northwestern Photographic Company of Chadron, Nebraska, produced the most important photographs, those of the dead at Wounded Knee. Ironically, this firm also stole other photographers' work, deliberately mislabeled images, and created

phony photographs to increase sales. Carter examines the economics of the small-town photography business and the varying roles played by the photographers who were associated with Pine Ridge and the Ghost Dance. He discusses the reporters, the relic hunters, and all the other characters who sought to make their fortunes from others' misfortunes. Yet his central subject is the photographic images that helped make Wounded Knee the symbol it has become. ¶ It has been easy for past scholars to become burdened by the symbolism of Wounded Knee and overlook the quirky details of the particular events and people involved. This book focuses on the details, as demonstrated by Jensen and Paul's text that accompanies the main body of photographs. The interpretation of the images has been the major goal of the researchers. They have sought to avoid a rehash of secondary sources, nor was a revisionist interpretation of Wounded Knee a justification for the book. It is not an evaluation of the historiography or a polemic. ¶ Though Wounded Knee took place in South Dakota, it is inextricably linked to Nebraska. The most important reporters were Nebraskans; the Nebraska National Guard was mobilized during the campaign; most of the U.S. Army troops and their supplies debarked from the railroad at Valentine, Gordon, Rushville, and Chadron; and the orders came in and the news stories went out on Nebraska telegraph lines. Most of the photographers who left us the images from those troubled times, and those of the stark and horrific battlefield, were from Nebraska. Having just marked the centennial of this most singular tragedy and the sesquicentennial of the invention of photography, we feel it is fitting that the Nebraska State Historical Society has prepared this work.

JAMES A. HANSON

Director, Nebraska State Historical Society

Chapter One

Another Look
at Wounded Knee

The Lakotas, or Sioux, first saw the high, rolling plains of western South Dakota a century before the massacre at Wounded Knee Creek. This proud, militaristic tribe had migrated out of Minnesota, forced the retreat of the Arikaras, Kiowas, Cheyennes, and Crows, and claimed this new homeland. The Sioux were divided into several confederated bands, or Council Fires, each of which occupied loosely defined areas of the new land. Among the larger bands were the Oglalas, Brules, Hunkpapas and Miniconjous. By the 1860s the Lakotas' old free life began to disappear as they felt the pressure of the numerically superior whites. The Lakotas had fought the U.S. Army to keep their freedom but after the Indians' victory on the Little Bighorn, the blue-clad soldiers seemed to be everywhere. At the same time, the buffalo, which had been the foundation of the Lakotas' economy since their migration to the plains, were vanishing. Prodded by the soldiers and faced with diminishing food sources, more and more Lakotas began to drift into the newly established reservations, live on government rations, and listen to a white agent tell them they must give up their old customs and religion and become farmers just like their white neighbors. ¶ In the summer of 1889, as the Lakotas' world seemed to be disintegrating, rumors circulated about a Messiah in the far west who had come to aid the Indians. Elaine Goodale, the supervisor of education in the Dakotas, was one of the first whites to take note of this Indian Messiah. In her diary, for July 23, 1889, she recorded a story told by Chasing Crane, who was just returning from a visit to the Rosebud Reservation. "He tells a strange story of the second appearing of Christ! God, he says, has appeared to the Crows! In the midst of a council he came from nowhere and announced himself as the Savior who came upon earth once and was killed by white men. He had

been grieved by the crying of parents for their children, and would let the sky down upon the earth and destroy the disobedient."[1] ¶ In September, Father Aemilius Perrig, a missionary at Rosebud, was told by a "Dakota Medicine man" that Jesus, crowned with thorns, had appeared to an Arapaho hunting party. Later in the month one of Perrig's students said that God had appeared to the Utes and warned them to beware of whites, not to believe them, and not to attend their schools or they would all perish.[2] ¶ The source of the rumors was a Paiute shaman, Wovoka, or Jack Wilson, who lived near the Walker Lake Reservation in western Nevada. In January of 1889 Wovoka had a great vision, which was the genesis of a religious movement that would become known as the Ghost Dance. Wovoka was ignored by the white world for almost two years, but his message spread rapidly through the Indian world by word of mouth, by letter, and finally by emissaries sent to Nevada from distant tribes.[3] ¶ In the fall of 1889 Good Thunder, Brave Bear, and perhaps four others slipped away from the Pine Ridge Reservation to investigate the rumors of the Messiah. They returned with the news that the Son of God was truly on earth and that this second coming was for the benefit of Indians, not whites. In the spring a second delegation, representing the Pine Ridge, Cheyenne River, and Rosebud reservations, left in search of additional information and corroboration. This larger delegation, which was sanctioned by some of the leading Lakota chiefs, visited Wovoka in Nevada. The travelers included Good Thunder, Short Bull, and Kicking Bear, who would become some of the most visible leaders of the Ghost Dance.[4] ¶ The second delegation returned in March of 1890 as confirmed disciples of Wovoka. Good Thunder went to the Pine Ridge Reservation to preach the new religion, while Short Bull went to Rosebud. They were

1. *Wovoka, or Jack Wilson (seated figure), was a Paiute shaman whose teachings formed the basis of a widespread Indian revitalization movement called the Ghost Dance.* ¶ Many Lakotas adopted the new religion and composed hymns sung at the ceremonies. In the following song, which summarizes the promises of the religion, sacred birds bring the message from the Father, or Messiah, of a renewed world, the return to life of a nation of dead ancestors, and the return of the buffalo.

The whole world is coming,
A nation is coming, a nation is coming,
The eagle has brought the message to the tribe.
The Father says so, the Father says so.
Over the whole earth they are coming,
The buffalo are coming, the buffalo are coming,
The crow has brought the message to the tribe,
The Father says so, the Father says so.
(James Mooney, The Ghost-Dance Religion and the Sioux Outbreak of 1890, 1072.)

2. Short Bull (left) and Kicking Bear were among the Lakotas who visited Wovoka early in 1890 and returned as confirmed disciples of the Ghost Dance religion. Like other native religions, it was banned by the Bureau of Indian Affairs. Short Bull warned his followers, "There may be soldiers surround you, but pay no attention to them, continue the dance. If the soldiers surround you four deep . . . some of them will drop dead, the rest will start to run . . . then you can do as you desire with them. Now you must know this, that all the soldiers and that [white] race will be dead." ("Report of Major General Miles," Sept. 14, 1891, *Report of the Secretary of War*, 142.)

quickly ordered by the agents to desist. Kicking Bear preached first at the Cheyenne River Reservation, where he attracted little attention, at least from agency officials. In October, at the invitation of Sitting Bull, he went to the Standing Rock Reservation, where he was expelled by the agent, but not until he had made many converts. Kicking Bear told the Hunkpapas, "My brothers, I bring to you the promise of a day in which there will be no white man to lay his hand on the bridle of the Indian's horse; when the red men of the prairie will rule the world. . . . I bring you word from your fathers the ghosts, that they are now marching to join you, led by the Messiah who came once to live on earth with the white man, but was cast out and killed by them." He then quoted Wovoka as saying, "The earth is getting old, and I will make it new for my chosen people, the Indians, who are to inhabit it, and among them will be all those of their ancestors who have died. . . . I will cover the earth with new soil to a depth of five times the height of a man, and under this new soil will be buried the whites. . . . The new lands will be covered with sweet-grass and running water and trees, and herds of buffalo and ponies will stray over it, that my red children may eat and drink, hunt and rejoice."[5]

The Ghost Dance, as outlined by Kicking Bear, offered a solution to the Lakotas' most pressing problems. With the disappearance of the whites there would no longer be bans on the old familiar Lakota religion and customs, and the Indians would again be free to pursue a lifestyle of their own choosing. The return of their dead ancestors would ensure the Lakotas the manpower necessary to protect their hunting grounds, bountifully replenished. Finally, the return of vast herds of buffalo would provide the necessary food and raw materials for the increased population. Of equal importance was the buffalo's key role in the Lakotas' traditional mythology and religion. The disappearance of the animal had left a spiritual void that would be filled when the animals returned. ¶ The Bureau of Indian Affairs could see the Ghost Dance only as a barbaric ritual and set out to abolish it. A typical opinion of the religion was offered by Standing Rock agent James McLaughlin, who called it an "absurd craze" and described the dance as "demoralizing, indecent and disgusting." He found no reason to change his opinion when he finally witnessed a dance a month after submitting his assessment. It seems unlikely that the ban had any effect on the spread of the religion. It is equally unlikely that the white officials recognized the irony of their actions. One of the primary duties of an agent was to eradicate native religious beliefs in favor of Christian dogma. With the spread of the Ghost Dance, increasing numbers of Indians professed a belief in the Christian God. Other important duties of the agent were to make the Indians take up farming and to educate the children. Wovoka's message to the delegation was clear on these points, for he told them, "When you get home, go to farming, and send all your children to school."[6] ¶ Settlers near the Lakota reservations demanded the suppression of the religion, for they were convinced it was a prelude to war or outbreak. On May 29, 1890, a citizen of Pierre, South Dakota, wrote what was probably the first letter to the Department of the Interior expressing this fear. Although the fear was unjustified, it grew to epidemic proportions after newspapers began publishing unverified stories about Indian "depredations."[7] ¶ The rituals of the Ghost Dance religion were becoming more common on the Pine Ridge Reservation by mid-June. In its basic form the ritual was a Paiute round dance, during which men and women formed a circle, held hands, and side-

3. The Ghost Dance ceremony and dogma were modified to fit the particular needs and religious frame of reference of the Indian tribes who adopted it. At the right in this photograph can be seen the sacred tree that was a characteristic of the old Lakota Sun Dance. A pole adorned with flags or streamers was sometimes used (see photo 5). J. E. Meddaugh photographed this Ghost Dance. It probably took place at No Water's camp north of the Pine Ridge Agency. ¶ By the time the dance had become a media event, visitors were usually not welcome and other photographers were not as successful as Meddaugh. Keeps the Battle told about a photographer, almost certainly Clarence Moreledge, who came to a ceremony on White Clay Creek. Keeps the Battle said, "This heap-much-dress-youth [Moreledge] came into the centre of our grave circle, and, taking a small brown box from under his arm, pointed a little hole in the end of it toward the leading Sioux men. A slight click was heard. . . . All of a sudden a boy who had been to Carlisle to school, sprang to his feet and cried: 'Etoape wachee!' (he takes picture). Instantly several men drew clubs, and, running toward the heap-much-dress-lad, struck the box from his trembling hands and smashed it to fragments on the ground." (W. Fletcher Johnson, Life of Sitting Bull and the History of the Indian War of 1890–91, 342–45.)

stepped to the left. To this completely foreign dance form, the Lakotas added familiar elements from their own religious rituals; thus the Ghost Dance became a part of the Lakotas' own evolving religion rather than a brief experiment with an exotic belief.[8] ¶ In the center of the circle of dancers, the Lakotas placed a sacred tree, or pole, festooned with offerings to God. A tree such as this had been part of the Sun Dance, the most sacred ceremony of the old Lakota religion, which had been banned by the Indian Bureau in the early 1880s. Dancers also looked toward the sun, another feature of the Sun Dance. Mary Collins, a missionary with long experience among the Lakotas, watched a dance and "came to the conclusion that the 'ghost dance' is nothing more than the old sun dance revived." With her experience, she may have understood that both dances were a means of obtaining supernatural aid, and not a prelude to war as so many whites suspected.[9] ¶ Other features of the Lakota version of the Ghost Dance had deep roots in their old traditions. Before the ceremony,

participants entered a sweat lodge. This purification ritual had been part of many of their old religious ceremonies. During the dance Lakota believers might experience a vision in which they saw the new world promised by Wovoka and talked to the ghosts of dead friends and relatives. Some of these visions were described in abbreviated form in the songs sung at later dances. ¶ The Lakotas, and most other tribes who adopted the new religion, wore a special Ghost Dance costume. A Pine Ridge Agency employee, Mrs. Z. A. Parker, described the costumes. "They were of white cotton cloth. The women's dress was . . . a loose robe with wide, flowing sleeves, painted blue in the neck . . . with moon, stars, birds, etc. interspersed with real feathers, painted on the waist and sleeves. . . . The ghost shirt for the men was made of the same material . . . painted blue around the neck and the whole garment was fantastically sprinkled with figures of birds, bows and arrows, sun, moon, and stars and everything they saw in nature. Down the outside of the sleeve were rows

4. This Ghost Dance scene was undoubtedly described by Sergeant George B. DuBois, who was stationed at Fort Yates. He wrote, "I have not seen the famous ghost dance and I dont believe any one els has if the press does say so. The dance of Sitting Bull is 38 miles from here and they will not allow any one within five hundred yards of it[.] an associated press reporter was the closest that any one has been here and he was about five hundred yards and took a snap shot with a Kodac for our photographer here [George Scott]. I saw the negative and will try and get one of the pictures if I can as I believe it is the only one taken of any of the dancers. It shows them dancing in a circle around a pole and one lonley teepy about forty yards from the circle. The medicine teepy I suppose and old [Sitting] Bull and two or three others are standing about half way between the teepy and the dancers. The Indians did not know that they were being taken in with a Kodac[;] if they did it would have went hard with the poor fellow." (Sergeant George B. DuBois to Private George Thomas, Dec. 3, 1890, MS no.215, box 1, Colorado Historical Society.) ¶ A Standing Rock Reservation schoolteacher, J. M. Carignan, identified the photographer as Chicago newspaperman Sam T. Clover, who surreptitiously took the picture with a camera concealed under his coat. Carignan adds that these were "the only pictures taken of the dance." (Frank Bennett Fiske, Life and Death of Sitting Bull, 35.)

5. Since photographers were rarely allowed to witness a Lakota Ghost Dance, there are very few unquestionable images of the ceremony. This photograph has been used to illustrate the dance, yet the costumes and the dance style are contrary to all the eyewitness descriptions. The image is probably of an Omaha Dance.

Below: Frederic Remington witnessed a Lakota Ghost Dance and his depiction is reasonably accurate. Although no Ghost Dance costumes are evident, he clearly shows both men and women dancing in a circle. Most newspaper illustrators preferred to show caricatures of armed men gyrating wildly.

Ghost shirts and dresses were specially prepared garments worn by adherents of the new religion. This example from the W. H. Over Museum has the painted V-shaped neck, fringes, and feathers typical of Lakota shirts. Only the Lakotas believed them to be bulletproof. Whites viewed this as evidence of the Lakotas' warlike intentions, choosing to ignore the primarily defensive character of a bulletproof garment. Although many Indians owned weapons, they would not be needed for an offensive war since the whites would disappear through supernatural means. ¶ Songs sung at the ceremonies included one about the Messiah's, or Father's, gift of the garments to the believers.

Verily, I have given you my strength,
Says the Father, says the Father.
The shirt will cause you to live,
Says the Father, says the Father.
(Mooney, The Ghost Dance, 1073).

of feathers tied by the quill ends and left to fly in the breeze." Mrs. Parker accurately described the shirts and dresses but failed to mention specifically the painted eagle found on nearly all surviving examples of Lakota garments, and that the blue neck was almost always in the shape of a deeply cut V. The painted birds, stars, and other figures represented scenes from the garment maker's vision rather than things seen in nature.[10] ¶ An individual might make his or her own garment or receive one as a gift. Holy Medicine was the tailor for Sitting Bull's Hunkpapas, whereas Mrs. Return From Scout served in a similar capacity for an Oglala village on White Clay Creek. Soldiers and tourists also wanted shirts as souvenirs of their visits to the reservations. A soldier at Pine Ridge observed, "Some old hag has got on to it and is making imitations for sale."[11] ¶ Although many Plains tribes embraced the Ghost Dance religion and wore the shirts, only the Lakotas believed the garments were bulletproof. The general concept was both old and

widespread on the plains, for warriors often invoked supernatural aid to protect them from an enemy's weapons. One example was the Omaha Dance, which had been part of a bulletproofing ceremony that the Lakotas adopted from the Omaha tribe.[12] In time, the ceremony was considered misused, the power was lost, and by 1890 the dance was merely a social function and a favorite subject of photographers. ¶ Some of the Lakota believers were not afraid to test the defensive properties of the shirts. Near the end of the fight that erupted after the killing of Sitting Bull, a Hunkpapa dancer rode boldly past the agency police and then past Capt. E. G. Fechet's soldiers. Although at least three volleys were fired, the Ghost Dancer was not harmed. Another test of the shirt was less convincing. Porcupine, a believer at Red Dog's camp, volunteered to ride a short distance from the camp, turn, and charge like an enemy while his friends fired a volley at him. The test was never completed, for as Porcupine mounted his horse, his gun acci-

6. George Trager's caption must have been written to help sell the photograph. The "Chief's" ghost shirt bears not the slightest resemblance to any surviving example or description. If this Crazy Bear was at Wounded Knee he survived, for a photograph was taken of him a few years later. (Ralph W. Andrews, Indians as the Westerners Saw Them, 77.) Joseph Horn Cloud listed another Crazy Bear as a Wounded Knee fatality.

dentally discharged and he shot himself in the leg. [13] ¶ During the summer and fall of 1890, the new religion spread across the Lakota reservations. There are no reliable figures on the number of converts, but perhaps one-third of the Lakotas were involved in the dance at some time. The Lower Brules were receptive but their agent put an end to the religion on the Lower Brule Reservation when he imprisoned seventeen dance leaders. About six hundred Hunkpapas under Sitting Bull were converts, but when the old leader was killed by agency police, the dance ended on the Standing Rock Reservation. On the Cheyenne River Reservation the Miniconjous, especially those with Big Foot and Hump, adopted the new religion. There were an estimated nine hundred converts by November, but soon the dance was rejected by Hump and nearly all of his people. The largest group of dancers, perhaps thirty-five hundred people, gathered in a section of the Badlands northwest of the Pine Ridge Agency that came to be known as the Stronghold. The majority were Brules from Rosebud, but many Oglalas from Pine Ridge were also present. [14] ¶ As more converts joined the Ghost Dance, the Indian agents' demands that the religious observances be stopped became increasingly adamant. On several occasions, beginning in late August, agents sent the reservation police to halt the dances. These confrontations had the potential to erupt into life-threatening riots, but the police, armed only with pistols, withdrew when they were met by resolute camp guards armed with rifles. At Rosebud, Special Agent E. B. Reynolds had to concede "that the matter is beyond the control of the police" and called for a "sufficient force of troops to prevent the outbreak which is imminent." The Cheyenne River agent, Perain P. Palmer, recommended the arrest of Big Foot, Hump, and other Ghost Dance leaders, presumably by the U.S. Army.

Of all the Lakota agents, Daniel F. Royer was the most insistent in his demands for military support. His pleas were taken seriously, and on November 18 the War Department had troops on the way to begin the military occupation of the reservations. [15] By the end of the month nearly a third of the U.S. Army was alerted for duty on the Lakota reservations. ¶ Although many whites were convinced that the Ghost Dancers were preparing for war, it is now evident that the dancers' primary concern was defending themselves from outside interference while continuing the ceremonies. First they abandoned their homes and retreated to increasingly isolated locations to avoid the army and the reservation police. When the police or any unwanted guests tried to interrupt a ceremony they were forced to withdraw from the dance camp by Ghost Dance guards. Once the intruders were out of the immediate area the guards also retreated. The bulletproof ghost shirts were consistent with this generally defensive posture. Elaine Goodale, who had worked on the reservation for five years, pointed out that the assertion that the shirts were bulletproof was not made until after the soldiers arrived. [16] ¶ The Lakotas began to divide into two factions after the first army units arrived on November 20. Agents were ordered to segregate the "well-disposed from the ill-disposed Indians." At the same time, the Ghost Dance leaders "notified all those who did not belong in the dance and would not join it, to stay at home or go to the agency." By November 24 there were 150 lodges of these "well-disposed," or "friendly" Lakotas camped near the east edge of the Pine Ridge Agency. The "ill-disposed," or "hostile," believers had been congregating in the northwestern part of the reservation near the Stronghold. Early in November, Agent Royer estimated the population of this group at fifteen hundred, but by the end of the month their numbers swelled with the addition of about two thousand Brules from the Rosebud Reservation.[17] ¶ Despite the attempted segregation, the line between believer and nonbeliever was never sharply drawn. Among the Indians who moved from the outlying districts to Pine Ridge Agency were sixty lodges (about 360 people) "of the turbulent ones, and some of them the ghost-dance fellows." This group camped west of the agency in the vicinity of Chief Red Cloud's home. The old Oglala leader claimed to be a nonbeliever, but his sympathies were clearly with the Ghost Dancers. His son, Jack Red Cloud, was a dance leader with a camp on White Clay Creek, but he moved with relative freedom between the believer and nonbeliever camps in an effort to maintain peaceful relationships, and perhaps to assess the strength and temperament of the army. On the Cheyenne River Reservation, the Miniconjou chief Hump became a devout Ghost Dancer. In early December he recanted, along with most of his followers. A few refused to renounce the religion and joined Big Foot's band.[18] ¶ After the army arrived, rumors and misunderstandings would influence many Lakota decisions concerning their interaction with the military. Based on the Indians' past experience with the military, some of the rumors were quite plausible and the Lakotas reacted to them, sometimes with disastrous results. Turning Hawk recalled that "while the soldiers were there there was constantly a great deal of false rumor flying back and forth." One of the first rumors to surface at Pine Ridge nearly caused the nonbelievers to flee to the camps of the Ghost Dancers. These Oglalas had heard that the army was going to take away all of their weapons. They were in the midst of striking their tents before government officials convinced them they had nothing to fear.[19] ¶ The flight of Crow Dog and his band from the Rosebud Reservation to the Stronghold was motivated, at least in part, by rumors and misunderstandings. Crow Dog said his troubles began when interpreters lied to his agent, telling the agent that the Ghost Dance was really a war dance. Agency officials then began to interrupt the ceremonies, so Crow Dog's band moved away from the agency. Then he heard that they were going to be disarmed and he said he knew this would cause trouble, "for whenever the government had taken anything away from the Indians it never gave it back or paid for it." At this point Crow Dog and his people left the Rosebud Reservation and moved to a Ghost Dance community on Wounded Knee Creek on the Pine Ridge Reservation, but there the agency police told Crow Dog that the army had arrived and was preparing to take them prisoner or kill them. After this they moved to the relative safety of the Stronghold.[20] ¶ Big Foot and his band of Miniconjou Ghost Dancers were subjected to similar kinds of misinformation that would bring them to the disaster on Wounded Knee Creek. Their dances began attracting attention in mid-September when a group of thirteen white squatters on the reservation petitioned for military protection. Among the signers was John Dunn, who would cause so much trouble for Big Foot three months later. On October 11 the Cheyenne River Reservation agent, Perain P. Palmer, reported that Big Foot's band was "becoming very much excited about the coming of a messiah." He added, "My police have been unable to prevent them from holding what they call ghost dances." Palmer also complained that nearly all of the dancers had Winchesters.[21] ¶ Big Foot and Hump, the two Miniconjou Ghost Dance leaders, were brought to the Cheyenne River Agency near the end of October for questioning. Big Foot was apparently the more skillful diplomat, for Agent Palmer was impressed with his friendly manner and his easy conversation. Palmer devoted

7, 8, 9, 10. *On August 9, 1890, the itinerant photographer J.C.H. Grabill traveled to the banks of the Cheyenne River. There he made at least four photographs of Big Foot and his people, who were camped along the river. By this time the band had probably adopted the Ghost Dance, but here the men are wearing the costumes of the social Omaha Dance. These pictures testify to the dramatic decline in the situation that soon occurred. Big Foot and his band mix freely with soldiers of the Eighth Cavalry from Camp Cheyenne. The soldiers are unarmed, yet at least one dancer brandishes a Winchester. In but a few short weeks such firearms would become a focus of concern among the white population.* ("Report of Major General Miles," Sept. 14, 1891, *Report of the Secretary of War*, 148.)

11. *Big Foot, or, as he was also known, Spotted Elk (front row seated, second from the left), was photographed by Smithsonian Institution photographer Thomas William Smillie on October 15, 1888, when he accompanied a delegation to Washington. Big Foot clung to the old Lakota traditions and resisted efforts by the Bureau of Indian Affairs to "civilize" him. He was not overtly hostile, preferring instead a kind of passive resistance and diplomacy of which he was apparently a master.*

much of his report of the interview to berating Hump, whom he called "the most dangerous character on this agency." As a means of putting an end to the Ghost Dance, the agent recommended that Hump be removed from the reservation, and then, almost as an afterthought, he included Big Foot.[22] ¶ As the Ghost Dances continued, the white squatters continued to pressure the agent for protection. On November 6 Palmer wrote a very mild letter to the commissioner of Indian affairs. He described the squatters as being "somewhat alarmed" and felt "it might be advisable to have a small detachment of troops sent here."[23] ¶ For several months, a part of the Eighth Cavalry had been scouting the general area from Camp Cheyenne, a temporary station only about fifteen miles west of Big Foot's village. Soldiers at this post had been ordered to "keep under restraint the Indians of Big Foot's following." Reports from camp led Brigadier General Thomas H. Ruger, commander of the Department of Dakota, to the conclusion that the Miniconjous were not an immediate threat.[24] Certainly the troops of the Eighth concurred, for they posed casually with Big Foot's people for photographs. ¶ After the army occupation, Colonel E. V. Sumner was placed in command of the military camp on the Cheyenne River, with orders to prevent Indians from leaving their home reservations. On December 8 the colonel met with Big Foot and the other chiefs in the area and found them to be "peaceably disposed and inclined to obey orders." At this same time, Hump was meeting with an old army friend, Captain Ezra P. Ewers, who convinced him to abandon the Ghost Dance. Big Foot thus became the sole leader of the Ghost Dancers on the Cheyenne River Reservation. On December 16 Colonel Sumner received the order to arrest him.[25] ¶ The day before, Big Foot's band had left their log cabin village to go to their agency at Fort Bennett for

rations. They reached Hump's village, where they learned that Sitting Bull, the Ghost Dance leader on the Standing Rock Reservation, had been killed by agency police on December 15. Many of Sitting Bull's followers had fled and sought refuge with Hump, perhaps not realizing that he was now an ex–Ghost Dancer. Big Foot offered to care for these refugees, but Hump would not allow it and threatened to send the army after him. Apparently, Big Foot decided to avoid any trouble, for he withdrew from Hump's village, canceled the trip to the agency, and returned to his home. Perhaps as many as forty of Sitting Bull's people and thirty believers from Hump's band went with him.[26] ¶ The retreat brought them directly to the waiting Eighth Cavalry. On December 21 Big Foot counseled with Colonel Sumner, who came away convinced that the Indians "were willing to do anything I wish," and boldly promised to "take the whole crowd" to Fort Meade as ordered. Before the end of the day Sumner's mood softened. He granted Big Foot's people permission to return to their village and accepted the chief's promise that the band would turn themselves in at Fort Bennett rather than go with Sumner to Fort Meade.[27] ¶ When Big Foot did not leave immediately for Bennett, the colonel became impatient and sent John Dunn to urge the Miniconjous on their way. Dunn was one of the squatters who had signed the petition asking for military protection, although he had been acquainted with the Indians for several years. Dewey Beard, one of the Indian survivors, later recalled the white man's message and quoted him as saying, "All the officers talk that they will catch all the Indian men tonight (not the women) and take them over to Fort Meade and then move you to an island in the ocean in the east." Dunn then urged the Indians to "[Go to Pine Ridge] right away if you want to save your lives. If you don't listen to me, you will get into trouble."[28] ¶ It was Dunn's story that set the band on the road to Wounded Knee. At first, Big Foot argued that they should stay in their village, but a growing number favored the move to Pine Ridge until finally Big Foot had to concede to the wishes of the majority. On the night of December 23, the band slipped out of their village, quietly eluding the soldiers. Later, Sumner complained bitterly that Dunn "got into their camp and told them I was on the road to attack and kill them all . . . so they just stampeded . . . traveling so fast I could not overtake them."[29] ¶ The band moved in a southerly direction, but when Big Foot caught pneumonia, the march slowed to a crawl; however, it was five days before the army could locate the Indians. On December 28 the band was confronted with Major Samuel M. Whitside's column of the Seventh Cavalry just northeast of Porcupine Butte. Although Big Foot carried a white flag, both sides formed a battle line. Big Foot moved forward and met with Whitside while nervous soldiers from both sides looked on. The colonel ordered the Indians to move to a camp prepared by the army on Wounded Knee Creek, and Big Foot readily agreed. When Whitside demanded twenty-five guns (apparently an arbitrary number), the chief was evasive but did promise to turn them over later.[30] ¶ That night more soldiers arrived at the camp on Wounded Knee Creek, and Hotchkiss cannons were positioned on a little hill northwest of the camp. Dewey Beard recalled, "There was a great uneasiness among the Indians all night," for they "were fearful that they were to be killed." The next morning the ranking military officer, Colonel James W. Forsyth, called a council. He ordered the Miniconjous to surrender all of their guns and told them they would be taken to another camp. Forsyth probably meant Gordon, Nebraska, where they would be taken by train to Omaha and kept until the Ghost Dance troubles were settled. Although their destination was not mentioned, some of the Indians misunderstood, and a rumor swirled around the council circle that they were to be taken to Indian Territory (present Oklahoma), which to the Miniconjous was worse than any prison. Charles Allen, a reporter who witnessed the incident, believed that if this point had been clarified "it might have altered the course of events" which led to the slaughter only moments later.[31] ¶ In grudging compliance with Forsyth's order, a few old weapons were surrendered, but the colonel believed the Indians were hiding their best guns and he ordered a search of the warriors and the camp. About this time another rumor began to circulate. The Indians had heard that after the disarmament, the soldiers were going to take the cartridges out of the guns, aim them at the Indians' foreheads, and pull the trigger.[32] ¶ One final misunderstanding, this time on the part of the army, convinced some of the soldiers that an outbreak was imminent. While a few soldiers rummaged through the Indians' tents for guns, an Indian in the council circle began singing Ghost Dance songs and, "stooping down, took some dirt and rose up facing the west . . . [and] cast the dirt with a circular motion of his hand toward the soldiers." Lieutenant John C. Gresham saw this and later expressed the majority opinion of the military. He believed the throwing of dirt was a signal to attack the troops, which the Indians had decided on the night before.[33] ¶ There were dissenting opinions, however. Lieutenant W. W. Robinson was convinced that the Indians did not plan to fight and therefore a signal was unnecessary. George Bartlett, a scout for General Brooke, considered the idea of a prearranged signal to be preposterous. Dewey Beard explained that the man threw the dirt "as they did in the ghost dance when they call[ed] for the Messiah." Rather than a signal, the action was a prayer.[34] ¶ Within seconds after the Indian threw the dirt into the air, a gun discharged, setting off the massacre. Black Coyote, sometimes called Black Fox, had refused to surrender his rifle to the soldiers and there ensued a struggle that resulted in an accidental gunshot. Almost immediately, fighting broke out on both sides. The few Indians who were still armed fought back, while others retrieved guns from the pile of confiscated weapons and joined the fighting. The shock, the surprise, and the pall of black-powder smoke that obscured much of the horror of these first few minutes of fighting probably resulted in more than half of the fatalities. Frog, who was in the council circle, said, "The firing was so fast and the smoke and dust so thick that I did not see much more until the fight was over." Elk Saw Him heard Black Coyote's gun discharge and recalled, "Firing followed then from all sides. I threw myself on the ground. Then I jumped up to run towards the Indian camp, but I was then and there shot down." Phillip Wells provided a lengthy and graphic description of his hand-to-hand struggle with a knife-wielding Miniconjou. Wells's nose was nearly cut off before he killed his adversary.[35] ¶ There were a number of neutrals who had come to see Big Foot's arrest. Newspaperman Charles Allen recalled their reaction after the first shot was fired. "As we turned to run, the first scene that had met our view showed the spectators, some in their buggies and others clambering in pell-mell, whipping their teams into a stampede . . . [as] stray bullets were whizzing among them."[36] ¶ Other noncombatants were less fortunate. Before the firing started, Lieutenant Robinson "observed the children, of all ages especially, playing among the tepees. . . . It was proof to me there was no hostile intent on the part of the Indians." Reporter Allen's attention

was drawn to a group of "eight or ten Indian boys dressed in the grey school uniforms of that period. The fun they were having as they played . . . carried the mind for a fleeting moment back to the days of boyhood." After the fighting stopped, Allen walked around "viewing the sad spectacle" and found "the prostrate bodies of all those fine little Indian boys, cold in death." George Sword, an Oglala, identified these boys as students of the Pine Ridge Agency boarding school who were returning from a vacation with relatives at the Cheyenne River Reservation.[37] ¶ In addition to the schoolboys, there were other visitors traveling with the band. Red Juniper, an Oglala, had been visiting relatives near Cherry Creek. She joined the band for the trip to Pine Ridge and was killed. Bad Spotted Eagle and his wife were Cree Indians on a visit to the Miniconjous. Both died at Wounded Knee Creek.[38] ¶ The deadly firing at the council circle lasted only about ten minutes before the Miniconjous began a full retreat. Most of them ran to the south across the Indian camp to the meager safety of a ravine. Many died there, including most of the women and children. Intermittent firing continued for several hours as the army pursued the fleeing Indians up the ravine and across the open countryside. Bodies were later found as far as three miles from the council circle.[39] ¶ As often happens in any disaster, some fortunate individuals narrowly missed becoming a fatality. High Horse was on scout duty for Big Foot while the band moved toward Pine Ridge. He blundered into an army camp, where he was arrested, and on the day of the massacre he was being escorted to the Cheyenne River Agency jail. Brown Dog had fled from the Standing Rock Reservation after Sitting Bull was killed. He wanted to join Big Foot's band but he had traveled too slowly to catch them before they reached Wounded Knee.[40] ¶ Most of Big Foot's followers were not so fortunate. On January 3, 1891, the army escorted a civilian burial party to Wounded Knee and 146 bodies were interred in a mass grave where the Hotchkiss cannon had raked the camp five days before. Seven more would die at the Pine Ridge Episcopal Church, which had been converted to an Indian hospital. The total number of fatalities was undoubtedly higher, for survivors and their friends removed some of the dead and dying before the burial party arrived. Joseph Horn Cloud listed the names of 186 dead. Later interviews with survivors by James McLaughlin[41] and others indicate that some casualties were overlooked by Horn Cloud. A total in excess of 250 is almost certain. ¶ By mid-afternoon the fighting on Wounded Knee Creek had come to an end. The army gathered up their dead and wounded and began the slow march back to the Pine Ridge Agency. They were accompanied by most of the Indian survivors, including about thirty seriously wounded who rode in army wagons. ¶ At the time of Wounded Knee the only other Ghost Dancers not under direct military control were the Brules and some Oglalas who had secured themselves in the Stronghold. Beginning in early December, Jack Red Cloud, who was a Ghost Dance leader, and other emissaries attempted to negotiate their surrender. In mid-December, Crow Dog and Two Strike broke camp and moved to the Pine Ridge Agency with about one-third of the thirty-five hundred "hostiles." When word of the slaughter at Wounded Knee reached the agency, these Indians fled back to the Stronghold. The Ghost Dancers under Big Road, Little Wound, and others who had been at the agency since the end of November went with them. ¶ Before the events at Wounded Knee, the Ghost Dance believers wanted only to be allowed to practice their religion without interference. After the Wounded Knee incident, some of them

took the offensive. They fired on the Pine Ridge Agency, fought the army near the Holy Rosary Catholic Mission, and attacked an army supply train near the mouth of Wounded Knee Creek. It was a futile effort, born of anger and frustration. By January 3 peace talks were again under way, and four days later the first large group under Big Road returned to the agency. During the next few days the most determined believers abandoned the Stronghold and came to the agency. On January 16 Kicking Bear surrendered his rifle to General Miles. ¶ In the weeks and months that followed, official reports were written and eyewitness accounts appeared in newspapers and, later, in books, describing the events at Wounded Knee. Since it was such a sudden and violent incident, it is not surprising that these accounts contain differences of detail and perspective. For the most part, there was general agreement on major events and personalities, yet there were oversights. Perhaps the most obvious was the identity of the Indian whose act of throwing the dirt in the air was interpreted by some of the soldiers as a prearranged signal for the Indians to attack. Despite the critical role of the dirt thrower, he was not identified at the time except as a "medicine man." A year later the ethnologist James Mooney came to Pine Ridge to do research for his classic monograph on the Ghost Dance and he identified the dirt thrower as Yellow Bird,[42] although this name does not appear in any known contemporary source on Wounded Knee. Since Mooney's time, authors of fictionalized as well as scholarly accounts of Wounded Knee have accepted his identification of the dirt thrower, but it is questionable. ¶ Philip Wells, a Sioux mixed-blood and army interpreter, was a Wounded Knee survivor. He described the man who threw the dirt, calling him "Sto-sa-yan-ka, meaning something straight and smooth." Another survivor, Elk Saw

Him, described "a rascally fellow" who was "making medicine" while the search for arms was proceeding. In this account the man's name was rendered Hose Yanka. Long Bull, a Miniconjou survivor, was interviewed by George H. Harries and told him that "Sits Straight (the medicine man) gave the signal to shoot." Later, Harries specifically identified the signal as throwing dust in the air.[43] ¶ Joseph Horn Cloud, a Wounded Knee survivor, said there were two men singing ghost songs. One was Shakes Bird, who apparently played a minor role, for he was outside of the council circle and not mentioned again except as a fatality. Horn Cloud said the other "Medicine Man was swinging his arms and singing Ghost Songs and marching around inside of the circle. He was a Rosebud Indian named Good Thunder. He was wounded. Afterwards he was an Episcopal preacher . . . for a while." Good Thunder was interviewed in 1912 by Walter Camp and admitted that he had been a Ghost Dancer and had been wounded at the mas-

sacre. His mother was a Brule and his father was a Miniconjou and, thus, it is probable that he would be referred to as a Rosebud Indian. He described the massacre but minimized his own role. He claimed that Black Coyote was the principal medicine man and that he also fired the first shot. Camp added that Good Thunder's nickname was Stosa Yanka, or Sits Up Straight.[44] ¶ From these eyewitness accounts it is apparent that Stosa Yanka, or Sits Up Straight, was the medicine man, yet James Mooney's interpretation has persisted. Mooney was told that the medicine man's son had been adopted by Lucy Arnold, a reservation school teacher, who knew the boy's parents and named him Herbert Yellow Bird. Philip Wells agreed that Arnold named the boy but claimed that no one knew who his parents were. Perhaps the misunderstanding about the boy's parents occurred because, at the time, there was a Pine Ridge storekeeper who was operating a kind of informal adoption agency. His name was Yellow Bird.[45]

"You are directed to send each of the Rosebud and
   Pine Ridge agencies two companies of infantry and
   one troop of cavalry. . . . As the Indians would
   not remain at the agencies in case of outbreak, the
   remainder of your command should be prepared
   to intercept any body of hostiles if they move west
   or south, taking advantage of the use of telegraph
   and railway."——Major General Nelson A. Miles to
Brigadier General John R. Brooke, Nov. 17, 1890.[1]

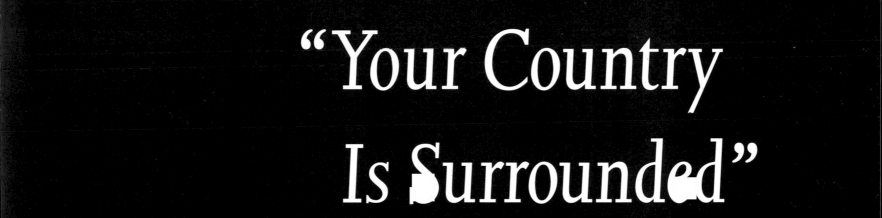

"Your Country
Is Surrounded"

The United States Army's role in the Ghost Dance troubles, familiar as it may seem, has been confused with those it played in earlier Indian wars. The events of 1890–91 have been mistakenly interpreted as the last Indian war, and Wounded Knee as the war's last battle.[2] The army's ability to respond quickly during episodes of civil turmoil had improved remarkably from the days of 1876. Railroad and telegraph lines now crisscrossed the Indians' former domain and linked military posts to one another and to their eastern headquarters. ¶ Improved transportation and communication had significantly changed the U.S. Army's strategy, especially toward the Sioux. Big forts with large garrisons now ringed the Sioux reservations. In Nebraska, for instance, Forts Robinson and Niobrara guarded the Oglalas and Brules at Pine Ridge and Rosebud. Fort Bennett, South Dakota, and Fort Yates, North Dakota, watched the Miniconjous and the Hunkpapas. Rail and telegraph lines served each fort, ensuring the swift response to a civil or military emergency. In the 1870s the Sioux were highly mobile, and the army operated from enclaves. In 1890 the reverse held true. ¶ The basic mission of the U.S. Army changed significantly between 1876 and 1890. Reservation Indians constituted just a few of the government's antagonists. Often enough, troops squared off against striking miners, riotous railway workers, and disgruntled war veterans, the former intent on upholding the law, restoring order, and protecting property. The regular army, along with the state militias, functioned more like policemen than Indian fighters.[3] ¶ If the army's role at the Pine Ridge Reservation is viewed from this perspective, then the "battle of Wounded Knee" becomes no battle. Two armies did not face one another that December morning, but rather policemen and dissidents, both armed. Each side exhibited poor

judgment prior to the outbreak of violence. Emotions overcame reason before and during the fighting, and innocent parties suffered the worst. Thereafter, this horrible day overshadowed the events that led to it. ¶ In short order, Wounded Knee entered the realm of myth. It came to symbolize the entire, wretched history of failed Indian-white relations. Meanwhile, the history of the Pine Ridge troubles of 1890–91 and the actions of its participants became obscured. The photographers of the "late war views" presented unforgettable images of the players. Yet, underrepresented by these photographers are such participants as soldiers debarking at the Rushville, Nebraska, depot (only two photographs exist) and telegraphers hammering out messages from the Pine Ridge Agency station (no photographs found to date). The railroad and telegraph, no myths but products of a modern, industrialized society, were intertwined with the military measures initiated to settle the disturbance on the reservations. ¶ The photographers made no effort to highlight these technological milestones of the modern army. They shared this shortcoming with nearly all participants and observers who at the time considered the events as merely a continuation of the Great Sioux War. Few saw parallels to other examples of civil disobedience and federal intervention of the 1880s and 1890s, especially with regard to the impressive military show of force. Only with one hundred years of perspective has the end of the Indian Wars been clearly delineated.[4] ¶ Little wonder such confusion existed. At first glance, the combatants of 1890 appeared unchanged from those of the 1870s. Familiar names from the Indian-fighting army littered the ranks, among them Miles, Carr, and Henry. Major General Nelson A. Miles had skirmished with Sitting Bull's band on the Yellowstone River in 1876 before its leader and a few followers escaped to

Canada. Colonel Eugene A. Carr had routed the Cheyennes at Summit Springs in 1869. Major Guy V. Henry, wounded at the Battle of the Rosebud in 1876, still bore the scars where a bullet from one of Crazy Horse's men had passed through both his cheeks. Cursory inspection of the 1890s soldier, with his dark blue uniform, single-shot Springfield, and silk guidon, revealed many similarities to his 1870s counterpart.[5] ¶ Fundamental changes had occurred, however, affecting both the U.S. Army and the Indian tribes. No "wild" Indians remained by 1890. They roamed the country only as actors in wild west shows rather than as members of hunting or war parties. Buffalo hunting had been replaced by beef issues on annuity days. All tribes had been restricted to carefully delineated reservations, marked not only by surveyed boundaries but also by the white settlers whose property abutted them on all sides. Tribes had become divided between those who did and those who did not accept change. Indian youths were sent to a variety of distant schools, like Carlisle, Haskell, Hampton, and Genoa, all with the purpose of teaching them to live like whites. The events of 1890–91 on Pine Ridge Reservation highlight these contrasts and demonstrate how far change had progressed. ¶ The frontier military posts, which now surrounded Sioux country, formed the first link in a chain of command that stretched to the White House. Forts Robinson and Niobrara were in the Department of the Platte, which was commanded by Brigadier General John R. Brooke from Omaha. The Departments of the Platte and Dakota defended the northern plains region of the Division of the Missouri, commanded by General Miles from Chicago. Miles reported to Major General John M. Schofield, the general of the army, in Washington. Schofield's superior was Redfield Proctor, the secretary of war, who had been appointed by President Benjamin

Harrison. Miles's movements along this chain between Washington, Chicago, and Pine Ridge attest to the speed and relative ease of travel that a military leader possessed by 1890. ¶ During an October swing through western army posts and agencies, General Miles came to Pine Ridge Agency. Miles saw the deteriorating situation for himself. He counseled with Sioux leaders, including American Horse, Sword, and Young Man Afraid of His Horses on October 28, and insisted they use their influence to persuade the others to abandon the Ghost Dance. Agent Daniel F. Royer reported by telegraph to his superior that the three opposed the Ghost Dance but believed that military action would be needed to suppress it. How much of this report reflected Royer's own views is not known. He had arrived for duty at the agency only three weeks before and had already suggested the use of troops to restore order.[6] ¶ By November the Ghost Dance movement among the Lakotas had assumed an alarming character. Special Agent E. B. Reynolds at Rosebud Agency reported, "Everything is being traded by the Indians for arms and ammunition," and he requested troops to prevent an exodus from the reservation. From the north of Pine Ridge and Rosebud came two troublesome, though not necessarily true, stories. Perain P. Palmer, agent for the Cheyenne River Reservation, reported that Captain A. G. Henissee of the Eighth U.S. Cavalry had told him that the Indians at the Cherry Creek camps were selling cattle to buy rifles and ammunition. Commented Palmer, "As long as Winchesters are among these Ghost excited Indians, the [Indian] police are powerless and can do nothing." He also thought that Sitting Bull's band at Standing Rock was preparing to leave the reservation, an act that was considered illegal.[7] ¶ Sitting Bull became the army's bogeyman of 1890, but his real influence remains questionable. Among his small band of immediate followers, it was considerable; among the Lakotas as a whole, considerably less. Nevertheless, the military authorities perceived him to be the grand orchestrator of the Ghost Dance.[8] ¶ Sitting Bull's career chafed the army. He had escaped to Canada in 1877, not returning to the United States until 1881. He toured with William F. "Buffalo Bill" Cody's Wild West show and had garnered great acclaim and attention. His recalcitrance, his unrepentance, and his avoidance of immediate, harsh punishment for his deeds in 1876 gained him no favors. The military hierarchy paid him an inordinate amount of attention, which rubbed off on his followers and one successor, Big Foot. ¶ By the second week of November the telegraph lines were humming. While ostensibly inspecting government beef cattle at the Rosebud Agency, Captain C. A. Earnest, Eighth Cavalry, observed a general withdrawal of traders, teachers, and mixed-bloods, with their families, from the outlying areas of the reservation to the safety of the agency. In a confidential report to General Brooke in Omaha, Earnest transmitted his findings from Rosebud. He interpreted this movement as a warning of impending trouble. General Miles sent Brigadier General Thomas H. Ruger, commander of the Department of Dakota, from his St. Paul, Minnesota, headquarters to investigate the Standing Rock Agency.[9] Decision making in Washington, however, was overtaking the events in the West. ¶ On November 13 President Harrison ordered the secretary of war, Redfield Proctor, to ready troops for the field. Harrison had received many reports from both the War and Interior departments. The Office of the Commissioner of Indian Affairs relayed its own concern, based on reports from Agent Royer and others, that an outbreak at Pine Ridge Reservation was imminent, stating, "It is not safe to longer withhold troops." The following day, without wait-

ing for Ruger's report, Schofield told Miles to "take such action as, in [your] judgement, may be necessary in view of the existing situation."[10] Though vague, Schofield's instructions allowed Miles to proceed with the mobilization and disposition of his troops. ¶ At the same time, General Brooke was receiving frantic messages from Royer, none more overwrought than a telegram of November 16: "Indians are wild and crazy over the ghost dance. . . . We are at the mercy of these crazy demons. We need the military and need them at once." Brooke countered with a request for the agent to list what "overt acts" against government authority had been committed. Although Royer replied that there had been several, he detailed only one, the unsuccessful attempt on November 11 to arrest Little, a Sioux man who had illegally killed agency cattle and dared the police to arrest him.[11] ¶ The Oglalas recognized the government's power. American Horse, who had prevented bloodshed during the attempted arrest, cautioned his hotspurs: "What will these brave words, brave deeds lead to in the end? How long can you hold out? Your country is surrounded with a network of railroads; thousands of white soldiers will be here within three days."[12] ¶ On November 17, the same day he ordered Brooke to the Pine Ridge and Rosebud agencies, Miles refused to divulge details to the press; technology had forced the army to change its tactics in dealing with Indians: "It would be unwise to say anything at this time. Anything I might say would be telegraphed over the country, and tomorrow would be in the Indian camps. The Indians now have young men who read English perfectly well, and they no longer depend upon runners to take their news from camp to camp. They utilize the mails, and keep posted with regard to current events affecting their interests."[13] ¶ On the evening of Tuesday, November 18, two special trains departed from Fort Omaha with the Second Infantry. At midnight Brooke followed in a private car. Quickly assembling his troops at the Fremont, Elkhorn and Missouri Valley railheads of Rushville and Valentine, Nebraska, Brooke marched to the Pine Ridge Agency during the night of November 19. Four companies of the Second Infantry, together with one company of the Eighth Infantry and three troops of the Ninth Cavalry from nearby Fort Robinson—about four hundred soldiers—made up this formidable column. Lieutenant Colonel A. T. Smith, with three companies of the Eighth Infantry and two troops of the Ninth Cavalry, left Fort Niobrara and arrived at Rosebud Agency at 3:45 A.M. after marching thirty miles.[14] ¶ Brooke's orders from Miles were to protect the agencies and to encourage the "loyal" faction of Sioux. Brooke also received the first of three similar cautionary—and fateful—orders from Miles: "One thing should be impressed upon all officers, never to allow their command to be mixed up with the Indians or taken at a disadvantage."[15] ¶ "Telephonic information" from Pine Ridge Agency indicated the Indians were not aware of the military's approach. Direct communication between Brooke and Miles was soon established with the repair by the army of a twenty-five-mile telegraph line from Rushville to Pine Ridge Agency. Western Union assisted by transferring two operators to Rushville to handle the extra messages. The Signal Corps began practicing with their heliograph, or signal mirror, system of communication, apparently with favorable results: "They can talk to one another at a distance of forty-five or fifty miles, which is about thirty miles better than the Indians can do."[16] ¶ Meanwhile, Miles continued to marshal his forces. He ordered Brigadier General Wesley Merritt, commander of the Department of the Missouri (not to be confused with the larger entity, the Division of

the Missouri), to ready the Seventh Cavalry and two of the light batteries of artillery at Fort Riley, Kansas. On November 21 General Schofield expanded this order to Merritt: "Have all the troops of your Department ready for movement by rail and for service in the field without delay." A companion telegram from Schofield to Brigadier General Alexander McDowell McCook, commander of the Department of Arizona, ordered the Sixth Cavalry mobilized. On November 22 Schofield informed Miles that cavalry stationed at Fort Leavenworth, Kansas, and Jefferson Barracks, outside of St. Louis, Missouri, were also available. Miles also received authority from Proctor and Schofield to enlist five hundred additional Indian scouts from among the "loyal and friendly Sioux."[17] The plan would encourage those Sioux friendly to the government and increase the native police force. The new recruits would be under the army's jurisdiction rather than that of the agent and his Indian police. ¶ The arrival of one group of Indians was eagerly awaited at Pine Ridge Agency. It was composed of the Sioux performers from Buffalo Bill's Wild West show, who were returning from a European tour. Led by Rocky Bear, they came directly from Washington, where they had been advised by Thomas J. Morgan, the commissioner of Indian affairs, to "exert their influence with their relatives and friends against an uprising or further fanatical demonstrations." En route to Nebraska on a special through coach, they were joined by C. H. Cressey, the correspondent for the *Omaha Bee*. He wrote, "They seem to a certain extent to realize the gravity of the situation, and it is believed they will do much toward restoring quiet. Several of the party had received letters from their friends at Pine Ridge speaking of the Christ and Messiah craze just before they sailed from Europe." Carl Smith, the *Omaha World-Herald* correspondent at Pine Ridge,

12. *The stagecoach moved people and mail from the railhead at Rushville to the Pine Ridge Agency.*

likewise noted, "All Bill Cody's Indians, past and present, are on the right side." Agent Royer thought so, too. He recruited several of the returning party of forty-five for the Indian police force.[18] ¶ On November 22 Schofield relayed to Miles another order from Harrison: "The President desires you rather to anticipate hostile action on the part of the Indians by precautionary movement to meet them than to delay movement of troops until the necessity becomes certain." Miles wasted no time. The Seventh Cavalry left Fort Riley the next day. Miles also moved troops to Rushville after hearing that the Brules of Rosebud were crossing the reservation boundary to Pine Ridge. The depar-

ture of as many as thirty-five hundred Brules eased tensions at Rosebud but created more problems at Pine Ridge.[19] ¶ A great army, the largest, said many, since the Civil War, was being gathered. On November 30 the Sixth Cavalry, stationed at its regimental headquarters at Fort Wingate, New Mexico, was ordered to Fort Meade, South Dakota. Its impressive troop train consisted of nineteen boxcars, twenty-eight stock cars, thirty "Teurist" cars, two Pullmans, and sixty-two cars containing forage for six days. The train held Colonel Eugene A. Carr, 21 officers, 450 men (eight companies), and all their horses and mules. It should come as no surprise that the largest expense of the Sioux cam-

13. Rocky Bear, here with Chief Red Cloud and Major John Burke, an associate of William F. Cody, led the Sioux performers known as "Buffalo Bill's Indians." They served as effective intermediaries between the military authorities and the Ghost Dancers.

14. The railroad moved the Seventh Cavalry from Fort Riley, Kansas, to Rushville, Nebraska, reaching it on November 26, 1890.

paign of 1890–91 was railroad transportation.[20] ¶ On December 1 General Schofield alerted three more regiments of infantry, including the First Infantry, stationed at Benicia Barracks, California, and the Seventh Infantry, at Fort Logan, Colorado. The Fifth Infantry, assigned to the Department of Texas, was readied but never took the field. The Seventh and the First left for the front on December 3 and 4. Miles also reassigned medical officers and hospital stewards from stations all over the nation and attached them to field service with the different regiments.[21] ¶ Miles and his Washington superiors did not believe they were overreacting. To emphasize Sioux determination, General Ruger reported that the Indians had been gathering and selling buffalo bones in order to buy ammunition. Cheyenne River Agency Farmer Narcisse Narcelle informed the agent that Big Foot had ordered his Ghost Dancers to obtain all the guns and ammunition possible. Miles observed, "There has never been a time when the Indians were as well armed and equipped for war as the present."[22] ¶ A key order from President Harrison on December 1 instructed Miles to "take every possible precaution to prevent an Indian outbreak, and to suppress it promptly if it comes."[23] If trouble came, it was to be confined to the reservation. This required a large force to cordon off the reservation and good communications. ¶ A military circular from Brooke to his officers reflected the army's strategy: "Every commanding officer will be strictly enjoined to detach couriers frequently, and report his movements, the direction taken by the Indians, and all important information, by the nearest telegraph line or other available means, reporting to his Department Commander, and other commanders, acting in concert, in order that they may all act intelligently, and that the Indians may be intercepted."[24] ¶ The Indians were not ignorant of the army's plan. One Indian, a spy sent from Fort Bennett to the camps of the Cherry Creek Ghost Dancers, saw "a number of educated Indians among the Cherry creek hostiles, who came to Pierre regularly every few days and bought copies of each daily paper on sale, which they took and read to a council composed of the chief and leading braves."[25] This confirmed Miles's earlier statement to the press. ¶ These and other newspaper readers across America learned of the government's efforts to settle the unrest peacefully. Sioux friendly to the military were rewarded when Miles hired dozens of Indian scouts. Their salaries of thirteen dollars per month plus rations promised to bring a tremendous influx of needed cash to the reservation. Simultaneously, the army used the Wild West show Indians to coax others who had fled the agency to return. By December 6 Brooke reported a successful council with Two Strike, a Ghost Dance leader: "While very much has been accomplished up to this time in avoiding loss of life, there is much more to be done."[26] ¶ The relative calm proved deceptive. The army remained apprehensive about the role Sitting Bull would play as a Ghost Dance leader on Standing Rock Reservation. On November 27 Buffalo Bill Cody arrived at the agency with the authority from Miles to arrest Sitting Bull, once a performer in Cody's show. The old scout-turned-actor hoped to visit the old warrior-turned-actor-turned-Ghost Dancer, gain his confidence, and persuade him to come to the agency, where he would be detained by the authorities. One could almost imagine how it would play before Cody's eastern audiences. ¶ The agent at Standing Rock, James McLaughlin, and the commanding officer at Fort Yates, Lieutenant Colonel William F. Drum, had no faith in Cody and sought to rescind the arrest orders. To buy time in which to plead their case with Washington, they employed a series of delaying tactics, including an abortive attempt to get Cody drunk, and, failing that, sending him on the wrong road to Sitting Bull's village. McLaughlin and Drum were successful, and Cody was recalled before he could reach Sitting Bull. His mission ended with his abrupt departure for Nebraska.[27] ¶ Within two weeks this slapstick episode was overshadowed when Miles sent an official arrest order to General Ruger: "You will now direct the commanding officer, Fort Yates, to consider it his especial duty to secure the person of Sitting Bull, using any practical means." McLaughlin was only too happy to assist. A squad of Indian police, backed up by two troops of cavalry and two artillery pieces, was sent out early on the morning of December 15 to carry out the order. The police rode ahead to Sitting Bull's cabin and made the arrest. Before they could spirit him away from the village, several of his followers became aroused. Sitting Bull harangued his people to save him. Shots were fired at the policemen, who then fatally shot their prisoner. A general melee broke out, during which the soldiers joined the fight and drove away the disciples of the dead Hunkpapa leader.[28] ¶ Word of Sitting Bull's death reached Pine Ridge within one day. The military authorities were surprised that the news of his death did not create the great stir that they had dreaded. On December 15 Brooke had reported, "All the Indians who can be brought in are now here or near here." His coaxing had worked, and to his astonishment, they stayed. General Merritt, interviewed in St. Louis, remarked, "I think if the report be true that Sitting Bull has been killed there will be no further trouble. . . . He was always a troublesome factor, and he has remained a menace since the Custer massacre." Agent Palmer reported to the commissioner of Indian affairs on December 17, "There is no longer any danger of trouble with any of the Indians on the reserve, except those belonging to Bigfoot's band. The Christian Indians are pleased with the news of Sitting Bull's fate and express a belief that the trouble will soon end." This may have been wishful thinking on the agent's part, but his report indicated that Big Foot had become the center of attention. Miles called Big Foot "one of the most defiant and threatening" Ghost Dance leaders, and considered his band "malcontents of the Sitting Bull fracas."[29] ¶ Unsure of Big Foot's intentions or those of another Miniconjou leader, Hump, Miles sought to keep them and the followers of Sitting Bull from going to Pine Ridge.[30] The situation was too volatile and the negotiations too delicate to allow the introduction of such a catalyst. ¶ Hump proved to be no problem after Miles ordered Captain Ezra P. Ewers, an old army friend of Hump's, to meet with the Miniconjou and persuade him to bring in his Ghost Dancers. It would have been impossible to arrange the meeting on such short notice—Ewers was then stationed in the Department of Texas—without the judicious use of the telegraph, by which Ewers was quickly tracked down, and without the railroad, which carried him hundreds of miles to the reservation. Within a few days of the order's issuance, Ewers met Hump, rekindled their friendship, and persuaded him to renounce the Ghost Dance.[31] ¶ Miles himself took full advantage of the railroad. He had traveled from his headquarters in Chicago on November 28 to confer with his superiors in Washington. He returned to Chicago on December 3. He decided to move closer to the action and left Chicago on December 13 for Rapid City, South Dakota. From there, beginning December 17, he communicated to his troops in the field and to those regiments yet en route.[32] ¶ The First Infantry typified the involved deployment of troops ordered by Miles in December 1890. On December 2 the regimental com-

Officers of 1st Infantry
Pine Ridge S.D. Jan 15th 1891

15. The rapid deployment of the First Infantry during December attested to the changes that the army had undergone. Stationed far from the plains, the regiment took only days, not weeks, to arrive where it was needed.

16. *General Miles and staff at mess, Pine Ridge Agency. Miles conducted the Sioux campaign of 1890–91 from his headquarters in Chicago as well as on the road between Washington, D.C., and Rapid City, South Dakota. Events at Wounded Knee forced him to take command in the field on December 31, 1890.*

mander, Colonel William R. Shafter, stationed at Benicia Barracks, on San Francisco Bay, received a telegram to prepare his troops for departure. The next day the orders came. The regiment left their post at 7:00 A.M., December 4, and took a ferry to Oakland, where a special train awaited. An uneventful trip, marked only by stops at Cheyenne, Wyoming, and Sidney, Nebraska, ended with the regiment's arrival at Valentine on December 9. Fort Niobrara became its temporary home, until the foot soldiers could be equipped and given mounts. On Christmas Day the First Infantry was ordered to take the train to Hermosa, South Dakota, and encamp. On December 29 it was given marching orders for "the unprotected settlements." At 10:00 P.M. that evening a courier brought them news of the Wounded Knee fight and orders to return to the railroad. The following day the regiment, along with General Miles, took a special train from Rapid City to Chadron.[33] ¶ Bad news from Wounded Knee had drawn General Miles to Pine Ridge. Before December 29, Miles's plans had appeared to be going smoothly. The Ghost Dancers abandoned their refuge, the Stronghold, for the agency. The *Omaha Bee* reported, "Within half an hour Miles' scouts and cavalry were in possession of their [the Indians'] natural strongholds, by the aid of railroads and telegraph and the unprecedented quick movement of troops around and all over the reservations." Lieutenant Colonel Sumner captured Big Foot on December 21, after it became clear that his band was leaving its reservation for Pine Ridge. General Ruger drew the obvious conclusion when he reported, "[This] practically ends the probability of any serious trouble with Indians of Cheyenne River and Standing Rock Reservations, and [is] a good step toward ending the whole trouble."[34] ¶ Unknown to the generals, however, Big Foot gave Sumner the slip on December 23 and headed

south. Miles feared his actions might "turn all the scale against the efforts . . . to avoid an Indian war." Through Brooke he sent out troops from the Sixth, Seventh, Eighth, and Ninth cavalry regiments to comb the country for Big Foot's band and prevent it from escaping into the Badlands.[35] On December 26 Major Samuel M. Whitside, with four troops of the Seventh Cavalry, two pieces of field artillery, and the scout Little Bat Garnier, was ordered to find Big Foot. Two days later he did. ¶ A flurry of telegrams told the tale of Big Foot's fate. Whitside reported the arrest to Brooke, who immediately relayed this important news to Miles. A wire to Washington prompted premature congratulations from General Schofield.[36] Brooke sent Colonel James W. Forsyth and four more troops of the Seventh Cavalry, a troop of Oglala scouts, and more artillery to reinforce Whitside. On Sunday evening, December 28, Forsyth arrived at the camps of Whitside and Big Foot along Wounded Knee Creek and, as senior officer, took command. By late Monday morning Forsyth was reporting to Brooke, through heliographs and couriers, the stunning news from Wounded Knee: while they were disarming Big Foot's band, a fight had begun. ¶ The firing could be heard at the agency, fifteen miles away, and created a furor among the Sioux camped nearby. Brooke wired to Miles Forsyth's message and one of Brooke's own that the agency was being fired on. Brooke followed with yet another telegram that had more details on the Wounded Knee fight. The report was grim: "I think very few Indians have escaped."[37] ¶ The world soon heard the news. By Monday evening the dependents of the Seventh cavalrymen were waiting at the Fort Riley telegraph station for details about the casualties.[38] Three newspaper correspondents who had accompanied the Seventh Cavalry sent their dispatches by horseback to Rushville. On Tuesday morning,

December 30, the first accounts of the incident at Wounded Knee appeared nationwide in the daily newspapers. ¶ That day brought another of Brooke's telegrams, with more details, some woefully incorrect: "The women and children broke for the hills when the fight commenced and comparatively few of them were hurt and few brought in." This may have prompted another ill-timed congratulatory telegram from General Schofield, this time to the Seventh Cavalry.[39] Having taken personal command at Pine Ridge, Miles now had more facts at hand and severe doubts concerning the accuracy of the initial accounts of the fight. He began to hear of the severe casualties suffered by noncombatants and suspected that soldier casualties had been due to poor placement of troops by Forsyth. Appropriately, Miles withheld Schofield's telegram to Forsyth. ¶ The telegraph lines, which had sung with urgent military dispatches, were now employed for the more somber events of the Wounded Knee aftermath. Friends of the killed and wounded soldiers were sought by telegraph. A casket was ordered for the remains of the only fatality among the officers, Captain George D. Wallace. The body was shipped by rail to his South Carolina hometown.[40] ¶ The "last Indian war" concluded within three weeks. The army evaporated almost as quickly as it had formed, ready to be reassembled for the next civil disturbance. W. L. Holloway, an author of a hurriedly pieced-together history of the Ghost Dance troubles published in 1891, proved to be its most perceptive military analyst. He wrote: "But forces were found at work with which the Indian had not hitherto called on to contend. The telegraph and the railroad have not hitherto counted as important factors. In this context, the click of the operator's instrument almost mingled with the rattle of the rifle shots. The railway whistle could almost be heard from the field of battle. The resources of the most powerful nation on earth were available in a few days."[41]

Chapter Three

Making Pictures for a News-Hungry Nation

The whole nation watched as tension mounted at Pine Ridge. It was the kind of story, rife with intrigue and the promise of bloodshed, that sold papers. It was a modern news story, with war correspondents from major newspapers and wire services on the scene, who kept the nation abreast of events as they happened. Photographers were there, too, because the public was hungry to see the incidents they were reading about. ¶ Over the years the pictures these photographers made to satisfy the needs of the moment drifted in to museums and historical societies, separated from the stream of events that caused them to be. The photographs of Pine Ridge ceased to be pictures of the "seat of war," as the reporters called it. Rather, they evolved into glimpses of reservation life. And the photographs of the people, particularly the Sioux, became historical and anthropological specimens, interesting more for what they revealed about clothing, art, and lifestyle than what they narrate about the unfolding of events. Separated from the immediacy of the incident that caused their creation, their significance dimmed with the passing of time. ¶ Some of the pictures developed new associations, ones never intended by their makers. These new meanings are equally disconnected from the occurrences. The historical accident of a blizzard two days following the massacre cast an icy specter that the camera recorded: people frozen in death, on a land frozen by cold, in pictures frozen in time. These battlefield scenes evolved into an evocative metaphor for the decline and destruction of an Indian culture, a vision of a vanishing race. ¶ But apart from the stream of events, these pictures are but fragments of a story. The intention of their makers was neither to document the systematic detribalization of the Indian, nor to show the grisly consequences of a failed, even malicious, government policy. These are stories

read into them later. Rather, they were created to feed the news-hungry public, a public little concerned with the photographs' potential importance to history. ¶ There are two contexts, then, in which these photographs are to be understood. The broader story is that of a national news event that fostered a clamor for pictures. The second, more specific story deals with the chain of events in northwestern Nebraska and southwestern South Dakota that caused these particular pictures to be made. ¶ In the years following the Civil War the nation's interest turned to its own expansive western frontier. Survey expeditions set out to chart and record the country's natural wonders, including its indigenous populations. Photographers went along and brought back glimpses of an unimaginable world. The pictures of Indians made by people like Timothy O'Sullivan, William Henry Jackson, and John C. Hillers excited the public's imagination. Like the photographers who revealed the exotic nations of China, Japan, Egypt, and India to the Victorian world, these early photographers who took pictures of American Indians brought to the Euro-American a wondrous yet alien people. ¶ Soon independent photographers discovered this taste for pictures of American Indians. But unlike the documentary photographers of the surveys, who worked for the federal government, the master that these independent photographers worked for was strictly profit. They learned to fabricate their pictures to meet the demands of the purchaser. In the world of photography of the American Indian, fact became subordinate to stereotype.[1] ¶ It is within this environment—a world of illusion—that the photographs of the Indian crisis of 1890–91 were produced. In all, there were five key photographers involved with photographing the Wounded Knee tragedy. George Trager, along with a number of business partners, is the

Two Strike & Crow Dogs Camp
Pine Ridge S.D.

key figure in the mass marketing of the Wounded Knee photographs. A young, adventurous photographer, Clarence Grant Moreledge, moved onto the Pine Ridge Agency and was there to take most of the pictures. Three other photographers, J.C.H. Grabill, W. R. Cross, and Solomon D. Butcher, arrived to take pictures after news of the massacre broke. ¶ The story of the Wounded Knee photographs begins with George (or Gustave, often called "Gus") Trager, together with his nephew Ernest Trager, business partner Fred Kuhn, and later partner Joseph Ford. George Trager was born in 1861, a native of Gefell, Germany. Prior to 1880, he emigrated to the United States with his parents and other family members and settled in Mazomanie, Wisconsin. In 1882, George went to Whitewater,

Wisconsin, to study photography. By 1888, he had opened a studio in Mazomanie with a partner, Frederick Kuhn. Information regarding this early period in their career is sketchy, but in the late 1880s, Trager and Kuhn left Wisconsin and meandered west.[2] ¶ In the fall of 1889 they arrived in Chadron, Nebraska, and there purchased the failing Bon Ton Art Gallery, operated by a Miss Alice Luce (or Luse). With markets that were easily saturated and an economy prone to dramatic fluctuation, making a living at photography in Nebraska was difficult. Luce kept her doors open scarcely a year before she sold to Trager and Kuhn, who attacked their new market with a vengeance. They aggressively advertised in the newspapers and expanded out of portraiture into scenic and landscape work.[3] ¶ The

17, 18. Clarence Moreledge's photograph of a Sioux camp shows a man, probably one of the Tragers, also photographing the camp.

TO SETTLE THE INDIAN TROUBLES

Send the Camera Fiends of the Eastern States to the Sioux Country by a Special Train.

New York World, *November 30, 1890.*

Fremont, Elkhorn and Missouri Valley Railroad transported people to the spas of Hot Springs, South Dakota, and the gold towns of Deadwood and Lead City, South Dakota. Because Chadron was a meal and lodging stop on this line, there was a market there for pictures of the American West. Tourists and adventure seekers poured through the city and were likely customers for views of the wild West surrounding Chadron, providing Trager and Kuhn with a constant supply of customers.[4] ¶ Within four months of their arrival, around February of 1890, Trager and Kuhn announced plans to expand their enterprise to Crawford, Nebraska, near Fort Robinson. It was at this time that George's twenty-four-year-old nephew, Ernest, joined the partnership. According to a newspaper account, Kuhn and

Ernest Trager went to Crawford, while George remained in Chadron to manage that business.[5] ¶ The hallmark of the Trager-Kuhn partnership was mobility. The local newspapers constantly reported their travels as the men photographed the town of Chadron, the countryside, local events, prominent or interesting people—anything that had the promise of a sale. Wherever there was a picture to be made, someone from the Trager and Kuhn studio was there to make it. ¶ Trager and Kuhn's wanderlust eventually drew them to the Pine Ridge Agency. On Monday, March 10, 1890, word came from the agency that the purported last live beef issue would take place on the following Wednesday, March 12. The issue of live beef had grown to be a popular spectator sport. Both residents and tourists alike traveled to the reservation to see cattle slaughtered in a mock hunt. The carnivallike atmosphere of the event, fueled with the belief that it would be the last of its kind, offered Trager a ready market for his pictures. This was Trager's introduction to life at the Pine Ridge Agency.[6] ¶ Through the spring and early summer of 1890 business was brisk; Trager and Kuhn continued to travel, and the volume of sales was good.[7] But the economy of the whole region was declining. In 1889 crops across the state had been bountiful, but the prices paid for those crops reached a record low. High interest on borrowed money and increasing transportation costs took a staggering toll on the income of both farmers and ranchers. The summer of 1890 saw a cataclysmic decline in rainfall to a level that had not been seen in twenty-five years. Crops failed disasterously and prices were low. A full-blown economic depression settled over the entire region. ¶ It takes little imagination to see the effect that this declining economy had on the business of photography. Photographs, a luxury at best, became a frivolity when money was scarce. Trager's only local competition had gone bankrupt in December of 1889—after being in business less than a month—and the convulsive economy placed increasing importance on photographic work other than the traditional business of studio portraiture. ¶ But a new opportunity emerged for Trager and Kuhn by mid-June. At that time the Ghost Dance appeared on Pine Ridge Reservation for the first time. On September 25, 1890, the *Chadron Democrat* reported, "The new dance among the Indians is . . . worth going miles to see." Like the beef issue, the Ghost Dance became an item of curiosity and entertainment for the local white population, at least for a short period of time. For two or three weeks people went to Pine Ridge and watched the dancing. Among the visitors was a photographer from Rushville, J. E. Meddaugh.[8] ¶ Meddaugh had a very short career spanning only a couple of years. While not involved in the Wounded Knee episode, he did make three pictures that are pivotal to the Wounded Knee story. During the brief period in which people could safely venture onto the reservation to watch the dancing, he went and made the only known photograph of the Lakotas doing the Ghost Dance at Pine Ridge. And two months later he made two photographs of the Seventh Cavalry debarking from the train at Rushville on their way to the Pine Ridge Agency.[9] ¶ It was fortunate that Meddaugh went to Pine Ridge when he did, because for the white population the tone of the events soon turned from amusing to sinister. By mid-November, stories of the dance and of rumors about the coming of a messiah filled the nation's newspapers as its citizens focused their attention on the otherwise unnewsworthy states of Nebraska and North and South Dakota. Fear spread that a general, bloody outbreak, like the one in Minnesota in 1862 (in which hundreds of whites were killed), would soon occur. ¶ George Trager, who was normally on top of any opportunity to sell pictures, was slow to capitalize on the burgeoning interest in the Ghost Dance. But his nephew Ernest fell victim to a serious case of mountain fever in early October, and it appears that George was obliged to spend time seeing to the affairs of the Crawford branch during his nephew's illness.[10] ¶ In early October the troubles at Pine Ridge were exacerbated by the arrival of the new Indian agent, Daniel Royer. His early reports to Washington intensified an already tense situation. Convinced that violent outbreak was imminent, he urged military intervention. Regular troops were dispatched from Fort Robinson, and on November 18 soldiers from Fort Omaha were sent as well. Two trains were assembled to transport the soldiers and their supplies to the reservation. The Omaha troops received a gala sendoff from a large crowd of family and well-wishers that formed at the station to cheer and sing patriotic songs. ¶ As the trains pulled out of Omaha, they carried not only the troops, but a group of newspaper reporters from around the country and forty-five Sioux who were returning home after a three-year tour of Europe with Buffalo Bill Cody. Among the dozen or so reporters on the trains were C. H. Cressey of the *Omaha Bee*, Carl Smith of the Omaha *World-Herald*, and a nineteen-year-old photographer, Clarence Grant Moreledge, who was probably in the employ of the *World-Herald*.[11] Smith and Cressey proved to be not only reporters of but catalysts for the events that followed their arrival. ¶ The *Omaha Bee* was a gossipy tabloid, strewn with stories about sex, violence, crime, and intrigue. In his first report, wired when he was en route to Pine Ridge from Cody, Nebraska, Cressey wrote about the Sioux who had been traveling with the Wild West show. His story hinted of dark and diabolic conversations and of their furtive glances out the windows and gestures toward the familiar landscapes that they had last seen three years previously. He interpreted these actions as a prelude to an Indian plot to attack the train at Valentine. There, confederates of the returning Sioux would join those on the train and thus begin the rumored revolution. This report was typical of ones that Cressey would later file. He depended on imagination, rumor, and hearsay to keep his stories exciting. Whether by assignment or disposition, Cressey's stories about Pine Ridge seethed with impending violence and conflict. His sensational accounts spread to newspapers around the nation and, amazingly, became a prime source of information about the Pine Ridge troubles.[12] ¶ The soldiers, newspaper reporters, and Indians arrived at Rush-

ville, Nebraska (the town and depot nearest to the Pine Ridge Agency) around one o'clock on the morning of November 20, 1890. There, to their collective surprise, they discovered Agent Royer. When asked why he was in Rushville (and not at Pine Ridge), he explained that he did not trust the security of his telephone and so came to town to send off dispatches. In his first report, Smith suggested that Royer was in town because he was afraid. That story ignited a personal battle between Smith and the agent, and, like Cressey's first story, set the tone for the reports that were to follow.[13] ¶ With the dawn of November 21, the reporters scrambled to secure horses for the trip to Pine Ridge. But when they got to the agency they found things to be astonishingly quiet. They also realized that the twenty-five-mile route between the Pine Ridge Agency and Rushville would become a painfully familiar one. There was no telegraph available at the agency, and the telephone was both slow and, for the most part, reserved for military use. Thus, to file their stories the reporters had to either ride to Rushville themselves or pay some local courier a handsome price to do it for them.[14] ¶ Word of the troop movements reached the nearby town of Chadron, Nebraska, and a party of "scouts and war correspondents" left that morning to see what was going on at the agency. The party consisted of Colonel Hugh D. Gallagher, the former agent supplanted by Royer; John Maher, a local businessman; C. W. Allen, the editor of the *Chadron Democrat*, who was also retained that day by the *New York Herald* to provide war reports; and photographer George Trager, armed with his camera. They stayed but a day, returning to Chadron on Saturday, November 22. Like most, they found that nothing was happening.[15] ¶ But Cressey was not there to report "nothing," and his imagination amplified the commonplace into the extraordinary. The Indian camps that encircled the agency in his stories became hostile forces holding the agency in a state of siege. While Cressey embellished his stories with half-truths, rumors, and outright fabrications, Smith harangued Royer with charges of cowardice and incompetence. These fantastic and accusatory reports from the two large state newspapers may have provided interesting reading, but they did not help matters.[16] ¶ The editors of both Chadron papers attacked the Omaha reporters for their sensationalism. Not only had the reporters caused greater tension on the reservation, but, more important, they scared off potential settlers. The situation grew so intolerable that the citizens of Chadron circulated a petition demanding that the *Bee* and *World-Herald* stop printing such incredible and provocative reports. "Although the protest will probably not do any good," reported the *Chadron Democrat*, "it is no doubt a move in the right direction, as the wholesale publication of outlandish and improbable falsehoods as have appeared in the state papers cannot but prove detrimental to this part of the country, and will be the means of retarding settlement for years to come. Let it be stopped at once."[17] ¶ On Tuesday, November 25, Trager returned with Allen to Pine Ridge, accompanied by the county treasurer and Colonel A. E. Sheldon, the editor of Chadron's other newspaper, the *Advocate*. Sheldon published the details of their journey and used the opportunity to lampoon Cressey's stories.

[We arrived at] the valley of the White Clay [Creek] . . . with hundreds of Indian tepees lighting up its banks with their watch fires, while beyond loomed the white tents of the Second infantry and the twinkling lights of the Agency buildings. It was evident that Pine Ridge was "surrounded" and the only question was how to cut our way through the hostile lines and relieve the hard-pressed garrison and war correspondents. The questions solved itself. A few minutes later we were clattering though an Indian village with dogs barking and the sound of children's voices and the hum of squaws as they busied themselves with primitive house-keeping, passed the camp of the Ninth cavalry with not so much as a "halt" from pickets, across White Clay creek and into the agency square, where an Indian policeman was pacing across the road and merely looked up to see that the rig was occupied by white men before resuming his walk. The siege of Pine Ridge was raised.[18]

Following their triumphant entry into the agency, the men made their way to the hotel, where they ate supper. After their meal they met Clem Davis, the agency's head farmer, who offered the travelers lodging for the night. The party was at the agency early the next morning to watch a beef issue. But Royer decided to withhold the beef as a means of coercing the Indians into submission, and so the issue failed to take place. That was all the excitement to be found at the agency that day.[19] ¶ Two days later Sheldon commented on the quiet at the agency in his report to the *Advocate*. "There was peace at Pine Ridge," he wrote, "whatever might be in the homes of frightened settlers and in the great newspaper offices." He also commented on the assortment of newspaper correspondents and photographers at the agency. His reference to photographers in the plural is significant. Certainly he referred to Trager, who was engaged in the lucrative activity of photographing the troops. Rushville photographer J. E. Meddaugh may well have followed the Seventh Cavalry to Pine Ridge after he had photographed them on November 26, and it is quite possible that Sheldon also referred to Clarence Moreledge.[20] ¶ Moreledge was living at the agency and was busy making pictures. During his first week, he made dozens of photographs of the agency buildings and grounds, the Indians, the soldiers, and the reporters. In one very early series of pictures he portrayed reporters William F. Kelley

19. C. H. Cressey (kneeling) and William F. Kelley (standing) in mock combat.

NO REPORTERS NEED APPLY.

(correspondent for the *Nebraska State Journal*) and C. H. Cressey in mock combat with an Indian. One of these pictures appeared as an engraving in the *Chicago Daily Inter-Ocean* of December 4, 1890, with the cut line "No Reporters Need Apply." ¶ The numerous photographs made between Friday, November 21, and Friday, November 28, 1890, began appearing as engravings in newspapers around the country the following week. The situation was quiet at Pine Ridge, but the war correspondents at the agency needed to justify their presence; pictures of the much-talked-about Pine Ridge and its environs made up for the absence of action. The lack of activity created the uneasy sense in many reporters that Agent Royer had protested too much. Not only was nothing happening then, but it appeared that nothing was going to happen at all. ¶ Yet the rumors of possible bloodshed persisted, for there was more at stake than the threat of Indian war. The soldiers provided a transfusion of cash into an otherwise dying economy. Carl Smith was typically blunt in his discussion of the economics of the situation. "The people here are making money out of the presence of the soldiery," he wrote. "Men who were glad three weeks ago to earn $1 a day now ask $5 for a three hours' ride with messages. I have just paid $4 for the use of a horse one night. These people and others do not want the troops to leave. All sorts of cock and bull stories are therefore palmed off as genuine and are persistently used by some of the boys. The hotel keeper here is making more money than he ever saw before, and he always has a wild, weird romance at his tongue's end."[21] ¶ Smith's frankness soon got him into trouble. From the day of his arrival at the agency, Royer had threatened to expel him, but every time Royer threatened Smith with banishment, Smith retaliated with a caustic personal attack. Finally, an article that was almost totally devoted to an indictment of

Royer resulted in Smith's ouster sometime around the first of December 1890.[22] ¶ But removing Smith and his incessant criticism from the agency did not eliminate Royer's problems. People were becoming suspicious of his motives in calling out the troops. Their presence needed justification, yet nothing happened. According to Smith's observation, "The situation is just this, the troops are here, having marched up the hill like the army of the king of France, and now it seems that there is nothing to do but to march down again. . . . The further one digs into this the more it appears that it is to be a serial story—the search for responsibility." The *Chadron Democrat* agreed, saying, "The situation seems to be that something must be done to excuse the coming of the troops here."[23] ¶ So by December 1 the newspapers and bureaucrats had created a chain of events from which there was no avenue of retreat. The local population exacerbated the situation because they wanted the troops, reporters, and other hangers-on with money to stay. At the same time, they did not want the situation to worsen, thereby driving off prospective settlers and investors. Neither was the profit potential of the situation wasted on the photographers at the scene. Trager returned to Chadron with a cache of photographs of the military, the Indians, and the beef issue, all of which sold well. And young Moreledge was doing a good business in providing illustrations for some of the newspapers.[24] ¶ But the contrived problems of a paranoid agent and inflammatory news reports did nothing to deal with the very real problems facing the Sioux at Pine Ridge. The pleasant weather of November turned cold in early December, and food was in short supply. ¶ The deteriorating situation inspired Trager to make another trip to the agency, this time in the company of J. L. Paul and J. M. Robinson. The local papers did not report the outcome of this trip, thereby suggesting nothing newsworthy occurred. Apprehension and boredom seemed to be the rule of the day at Pine Ridge at the onset of the Christmas season.[25] ¶ The death of Sitting Bull and the subsequent flight of Big Foot's band shattered the fragile calm, but military actions, culminating in Big Foot's surrender, brought a tenuous equilibrium. The newspapers of December 29, 1890, all but universally proclaimed the situation resolved. But peace was short-lived, for while the nation read about the end of the problem, the fighting and killing at Wounded Knee Creek was taking place. ¶ Brief and sketchy reports of the fight reached Chadron by Tuesday morning, December 30. On learning of the conflict, a delegation of citizens set upon General Miles immediately on his arrival in the city at noon of that day, requesting a pass to visit Pine Ridge to gather information. Miles acceded to their request. A party made up of Will Hayword, F. B. Carly, E. E. Egan, A. E. Sheldon, William Jones (who operated the daily stagecoach line to Pine Ridge), and George Trager prepared to set out for the reservation.[26] ¶ C. W. Allen, previously a member of such parties, was already on the reservation. Allen, Cressey, and William Kelley were at Wounded Knee and had witnessed the bloodshed. Allen had been in the Indian camp when the firing began and avoided injury only by crawling on his stomach up the embankment to the relative safety of the gun emplacements. Cressey had been with the cannoneers and out of harm's way. Kelley had participated actively in the fight, taking the rifle of a fallen soldier and firing on the Indians.[27] ¶ The group from Chadron did not leave for Pine Ridge, twenty-five miles away, until four o'clock that afternoon. Heading north and east toward the Beaver Creek valley, Sheldon reported that they met a "continuous stream of fugitive humanity" en route, refugees fleeing in the face of reports of all-out war.[28] ¶ As darkness fell, the group arrived at the Adaton post office on Beaver Creek, about half-way to the reservation. They changed horses there, had a meal of cold roast beef sandwiches and hot coffee, and listened to chilling stories told by the young man in charge. ¶ Armed with five rifles and a revolver, the group decided to continue to the agency under the cover of darkness, in the belief that the Sioux would not attack at night. All of the lighthearted nature of the trip of a month earlier was gone. For all they knew, a war was on and they could well be riding into mortal danger. Trager cursed his luck for having failed to bring along any liquor with which to bolster his courage, a sentiment seconded by a number of his companions.[29] ¶ The party traveled with guns in hand and watched intently for any sign of trouble. The moon rose as they neared the reservation, and they could see what appeared to be a burning building in the distance. About three miles from the agency the road dipped into a ravine, which, all agreed, was a good site for an ambush, and with anxieties running high, Jones pushed the horses faster. There was no ambush as the party passed through the ravine, and they sighed with relief as they cleared the area and came upon a picket line thrown up across the road. Soldiers constructing breastworks greeted them. Observing the sweat of their horses and the general agitation of the travelers, one trooper laconically quipped, "Good leather, boys," as he let the group pass. No one laughed.[30] ¶ As the wagon forded White Clay Creek and entered the agency square they passed the remnants of Big Foot's band, huddled together, cold, hungry, tired, and shell-shocked. Once again the Chadron contingent imposed on Clem Davis's hospitality. The men stayed up until two o'clock in the morning listening to Davis recount the events of the previous two days.[31] ¶ The next morning the group visited the

Episcopal church, which had been pressed into service as a hospital. It is likely that this is when Trager made the pictures of the hospital's interior (Plates 88 and 89). That day, December 31, a blizzard struck, confining activities to the agency grounds. But in the afternoon, despite the cold and snow, the Chadronites witnessed the funeral services for the soldiers who were killed in the fight.[32] ¶ The weather cleared at eleven o'clock the following morning, January 1, 1891, and a reconnaissance party of Indians went to the site of the massacre. They were fired on and returned to the agency. Two days later, a detachment of soldiers accompanied a hired civilian burial detail to the battlefield. Trager, with his camera, was in that company.[33] ¶ While the detail collected the dead and dug the mass grave, Trager made photographs. Evidence in the photographs suggests that another photographer, probably Moreledge, accompanied and assisted Trager. As noted earlier, Moreledge was at the reservation and certainly by this time knew Trager. Further, one of the photographs of the dead lying on the battlefield carries a number consistent with Moreledge's filing system (about which more will be said below). But the most compelling proof of the presence of a second photographer is found in one of the battlefield scenes (Plate 64) which shows a second photographer standing by a camera. ¶ Among the others who went to the battle site was Joe Ford. It appears that he and Trager struck up a partnership there. Ford was an energetic man with a powerful drive for success. He had moved to Chadron from Buffalo Gap, South Dakota, in the spring of 1888 and opened an auction service, pawnshop, and barbershop there. In late 1889 he joined with H. D. Mead to open an "Auction, Second Hand and Commission House" next door to the M. E. Smith and Company store.[34] ¶ Ford did well. Within a year he expanded his barber shop to

three chairs and added public baths. Around December 1, 1890, he opened a barber shop at Pine Ridge Agency, which was an immediate success, no doubt due to the glut of troops, reporters, and others lingering at the agency, waiting for something to happen. While not at the Wounded Knee battlefield, Ford was with a Hotchkiss detachment at the agency when it was fired on.[35] ¶ While Trager was taking pictures, Ford joined the host of scavengers collecting "relics." The Chadronites, including Ford and C. W. Allen, returned home on Monday, January 5. Trager took his valuable collection of glass plates and Ford and Allen their battlefield mementos.[36] ¶ The next day, Tuesday, January 6, Trager, Ford, and Allen went back to the agency. Although the battle was over, the situation there was tense. On this day, another photographer arrived.[37] Solomon D. Butcher was at that time living in West Union, Nebraska. West Union, a small town in the central part of the state, was more than two hundred miles from Pine Ridge. Butcher was a self-proclaimed historian with a camera, an itinerant photographer desperately trying to make a living from his craft. ¶ Butcher had a taste for get-rich-quick schemes, and with cash scarce, he saw the events at Pine Ridge as an unquestionable opportunity. In the company of Henry C. Orvis, also of West Union, he set out for the agency, arriving there on January 6, the same day as Trager, Ford, and Allen. Butcher and Orvis remained there until the following Sunday, January 11.[38] ¶ Although Butcher claimed having "over forty" views, the back list found on extant pictures contains those numbered one through seventeen and also number thirty-six. Of Butcher's known Pine Ridge pictures, none are numbered (outside of the advertised ones) beyond number seventeen. The other twenty or so to which he refers are probably pirated from other photographers at the scene.[39]

¶ Despite his claim that the pictures were worth "thousands of dollars," Butcher's images are of little consequence. Their quality, particularly when compared with the other photographs generated at the same time, is at best second-rate and their content is minimal. He simply did not visit the places where the events took place and never photographed anyone of significance. In fact, Butcher is worthy of mention only because his work contributed to the confusion as to who actually took what pictures. ¶ During that first week of January 1891, Trager and Ford, together with Clarence Moreledge, were the center of photographic activity. Trager and Ford, no doubt aware that they had negatives worth thousands of dollars, began to consolidate their enterprises. On returning from Pine Ridge on January 8, Ford arranged to sell his barber shop to Otto Gillam, an employee.[40] ¶ Trager bought out the interest of his partner, Fred Kuhn, on January 1. They also closed the Crawford studio on that day, so it is possible that the dissolution of the partnership had been in the works for some time. Certainly the economy may have doomed the enterprise, and, after a number of years of partnership, it is possible that Kuhn may have wanted to go his own way. He may, in fact, have left town altogether, as his name never again appears in the local papers.[41] ¶ With these business matters completed, Trager and Ford moved their enterprise into high gear. Trager commuted constantly between Chadron and Pine Ridge. "G. E. Trager came over from the Agency Tuesday evening," reported the *Chadron Democrat* on January 15, 1891, "but as he went back yesterday [Wednesday, January 14] without hardly saying 'boo' to Chadron people leads us to believe there is not particular danger over there, and no news of very great importance, but it indicates that Gus is doing a rushing business." Indeed he was. ¶ With George

Trager and Joe Ford traveling constantly, and Ernest Trager closing out the business in Crawford to move to Chadron to supervise the large-scale printing of the Wounded Knee negatives, little time was available to sell the pictures. Arrangements were quickly made with the store next door to Ford's auction house, M. E. Smith and Company, to market the pictures locally. The newspaper article announcing the arrangement recommended, "There are a number of beauties among them, and are just the thing to send to your friends back east." Finally Trager had found something to bring coins out of the tight local purses.[42] ¶ The Smith Company, too, found the arrangement a good one. On January 16 they took out a quarter-page advertisement. This is a very important advertisement, for it indicates that Trager had either purchased or in some way made arrangements to use Clarence Moreledge's negatives. A collaboration would be the logical conclusion. Trager made pictures on tiring, day-long, excursions from Chadron, while Moreledge, already at the agency with little to do, photographed freely. Thus Trager was not able to make the "hundreds of views" referred to in the advertisement, as Moreledge had, and yet pictures clearly attributable to Moreledge appear on Trager mounts. ¶ Moreledge's photographs are distinctive. They each bear his "CGM" monogram, executed in India ink on the negative, appearing in white on the print. They all bear a four-digit number, ranging between one thousand and sixteen hundred. These numbers were sequentially assigned by Moreledge, and for the most part, they follow the chronology of events. Many pictures display a second two- or three-digit number. These numbers correspond to envelopes in which they were kept by Trager.[43] ¶ Although Moreledge sold some of his pictures before the massacre to illustrated newspapers for reproduction as engrav-

20. Photograph by Solomon D. Butcher entitled "No. 3—Cheyenne Squaw and papoose, school in the distance."

Below, *The Chadron Advocate*, Friday, January 16, 1891.

After the "Barbecue" 4th of July, A.D. 1891, P.R. Agency, S.D.

No. 1589

21. This photograph, made on the 4th of July, 1891, was one of Moreledge's last at the Pine Ridge Agency. It shows both the number, 1589, which he sequentially assigned to his pictures and his distinctive C. G. M. monogram.

ings, he had neither the facilities to print the volume of pictures that the market demanded nor the Chadron storefront from which to sell them. He had the negatives and Trager had the facilities. ¶ Moreledge was young and reckless. His bravado was an asset that carried him into situations that mature and reasoned persons most likely would have avoided. Thus he obtained pictures that others could not. Carl Smith, returned to Pine Ridge from exile, commented on Moreledge's reckless abandon.

General Miles having issued an order that no reporters communicate with the hostile Indians, it became necessary for the World-Herald correspondent to become a photographer so as to get within hearing distance of the camp. A boyish young button presser named Clarence Moreledge, who came from Omaha and who has more nerve than a grown man, secured a pass for the photographic party. The photograph party consisted of the two of us, I lugging the three-legged thing which he was to level on the ghost dancers. The sentinel at the top of the hill stopped us and gave us the cheerful information that we were damned fools. ¶ The camp was but a mile away and we could plainly see the Indians and ponies on the hills and the tepees in the val ley. There looked to be a million and I was glad of a case of pleuritic rheumatism which supplied an excuse for causing Moreledge to hold back and go with less precipitation. ¶ Half way down in the valley we came upon a deserted house. An old French woman named Merville had occupied it, but there was nobody to answer our knocks. We pottered around awhile and the old man [Mrs. Merville's husband], who was in a far corner of the valley looking for ponies, galloped up. ¶ "Yo tek too beg reesk," he shouted. "Yo get kill dam dead." I didn't like that, but Moreledge seemed to regard the information as being below par. We pitched the camera on the top of a barn and Moreledge started in to training it. As he did so there seemed to be some sort of commotion on the hillside. Five or six horsemen hurried down the road, several pedestrians with the long, swinging walk peculiar to Indians, followed. It made one very tired, but the photographer kept right at it. ¶ As he worked old man Merville pointed out the ruins of a straw stack which the Indians half a mile away had burned. Looking back the way we had come, I saw the blamed sentry had disappeared. Luck gave us more nerve and we decided that the Indians who were rustling along the creek bank to our left meant no harm to us. The picture man wanted a closer view. We decided to go into the camp, or as near as we could. We walked around up the right bank of the wide ravine, the artist, I am bound to say, ahead. ¶ In the space of time, which seemed lamentably short, we came upon two of the Indians who had evidently left the camp to see what we were about. ¶ The photographer said something outlandish which was supposed to be indicative of our errand. Then he pointed to me and to himself and made a motion like the shooting of a gun [asking if the Indian intended to shoot the two of them]. ¶ The Indians said "yes," which chilled us some. But Moreledge wanted a picture very bad, and he tried again showing the Indian some money. The Sioux grabbed the money, saying "no, no, no," and started away with it. He meant that we would not be shot, just as he had before meant that we would. ¶ It was horse and horse, so Moreledge thought we would better go over to the camp. After a little walk past several tramp Indians a stop was made at the

suggestion of the Indian, for it had been decreed by the general [Miles] that under no circumstances should a white man be allowed clear in. ¶ The edge of the camp had been reached and I judged that if there was any danger, it would have before made its appearance. But there was none. The Indians gathered around and told the photographer to hurry up, and he did, too. ¶ The visit resulted in no accomplishment other than the securing of a good negative and the discovery that a number of Indians wore arms.[44]

Chadron was one of several hot markets for the photographs that Trager and Moreledge made. The lucrative market among the soldiers garrisoned at Pine Ridge inspired Trager to make frequent trips. The national attention focused on Pine Ridge made heroes of all of the soldiers, attention that created a booming market for pictures of the various military units involved. In a letter to his wife, dated January 11, 1891, Lieutenant Alexander R. Piper of the Eighth Infantry describes this frenzy for pictures.

At 8:30 this a.m. we, "C" Company, had our pictures taken. I think it will make a fine picture. The Hotchkiss gun is in the foreground, the men in a half circle sitting and standing on the earthworks, and in the background Red Cloud's house. The picture will not be ready for distribution before February 10th. ¶ I have ordered 40 for the company. They will be as large as our Class picture and will cost only 50c. The men have signed up for what they want and I have put down for three. That's enough, don't you think so? If we want more later we can get them at the same price. The men were just tickled to death over it.[45]

At fifty cents per picture, this one order brought the photographer twenty dollars. This sale certainly looked good in an area where it was reported only a few months earlier that people were grateful to earn one dollar per day. And the soldiers were not the only people who wanted these pic-

22, 23. There is no better example of Trager's willingness to compromise fact in the interest of sales than this pair of photographs. The man pictured is a Kiowa named *Apiatan*, who visited the Pine Ridge area in late 1890 and early 1891. During the unrest, newspapers were full of stories involving *Young Man Afraid of His Horses*—a man with features far less striking than those of *Apiatan*. On a number of the photographs that Trager sold of the Kiowa, he identified him as *Young Man Afraid of His Horses*, who, to Trager, looked the part of the "Chief of all the Sioux."

24. Nothing demonstrates better the market-driven nature of the photographers than the outright frauds committed by George Trager. This photograph and the following article from the Chadron Advocate of March 13, 1891, make the point well:
¶ George Stover and Bill Hudspeth were in this week from the White River country. We have a good story on Bill. . . . [A photo] of Hudspeth's boy in Indian costume taken a few weeks ago has been labelled "The youngest son of Chief Two Strikes" by Artist Trager and is selling all over the East like water melons at a colored camp meeting. The writer was showing said picture to friends in South Nebraska a few days ago when one young lady exclaimed, "What a cruel, vindictive face that boy has—just like his old villain father."

25. No better example exists of J.C.H. Grabill's inherent sense of beauty and grace than
this pastoral view of a Sioux camp.

tures; Trager sold them to curious civilians back at Chadron.[46] ¶ The demand for pictures drew two other photographers to the Pine Ridge Agency: J.C.H. Grabill and W. R. Cross. Grabill had studios in Deadwood and Lead City, South Dakota, and Cross was from Hot Springs, South Dakota. Grabill had established himself in Deadwood in 1888, photographing mining and railroad activities in the area. He had some previous experience photographing Indians, most notably a series of photographs of Big Foot's band dancing at the Cheyenne River Agency, taken in August of 1890.[47] ¶ Cross had considerable experience photographing Indians. He had come to Omaha, Nebraska, around 1867 and established a studio there. In 1870 he joined a land company and became a founder of the town of Creighton, Nebraska. Later he moved to Niobrara, Nebraska, where he continued to operate as a photographer. He was probably the photographer who made the stereo views of Sitting Bull and his followers during their incarceration at Fort Randall in 1886; these pictures sold under the names of Bailey, Dix, and Mead, the men who commissioned the photographs.[48] ¶ Cross later moved to Fort Niobrara, Nebraska, where he worked for several years. It was there that he took on a young apprentice, John A. Anderson, who later became a significant photographer of the Sioux at the Rosebud Agency. He later sold his Fort Niobrara studio to Anderson and moved to Hot Springs in 1889.[49] ¶ Both Grabill and Cross appeared at Pine Ridge at the same time, around January 16, 1891. Surprisingly, neither the Hot Springs paper nor the one at Deadwood carried any mention of the activities of either photographer, in stark contrast to the Chadron papers, which carefully followed every move that Trager and his associates made. For this reason, there is little hard evidence of their activities, save for that found in the pictures themselves.

Grabill rarely dated his images with more than the copyright year of 1891, although he applied specific dates to a few, with the earliest appearing on January 16, and the latest on the nineteenth. Cross was somewhat better, dating his images from the seventeenth through the nineteenth. ¶ Grabill's photographs are noteworthy not because their content is particularly important, but because they are so excellently crafted. He possessed a keen sense of composition and was able to produce prints of superior quality. Even mundane pictures of groups of people are rendered in a fashion pleasing to the eye. ¶ Cross was a less gifted photographer, and his prints, although interesting, are nothing worthy of particular note. What is interesting is that many of them parallel those made by Grabill (compare plate 25, by Grabill, below, with plate 111, by Cross). The similarities suggest that the two traveled together and shot roughly the same scenes. There is no indication that either photographer remained in the area beyond January 21. Certainly by that date, three weeks after the fight, activities at the agency were almost back to normal. The government had replaced Agent Royer with a military officer, Sitting Bull was dead, Big Foot was dead and his band decimated, and newspaper correspondents were banned from contact with the Indians.[50] ¶ The onset of peace meant the end of the story so far as the newspapers were concerned, so late January was also when most of the correspondents returned home. They had reported their war and other news was breaking. ¶ The newsworthiness of the event may have waned, but the demand for the pictures being sold by Trager and Ford had not. Sometime before January 29, Trager and Ford established the Northwestern Photographic Company, for the purpose of selling their Pine Ridge views. Trager and Ford added a new partner, W. W. Hayword, to their enterprise. It seems, although not stated explicitly, that his one-quarter interest came from a cash investment.[51] ¶ The Northwestern Photographic Company advertised a line of over two hundred views related to the recent unrest (probably incorporating those by Clarence Moreledge), which, according to Ford, sold "like hotcakes." During the week of January 26, a delegation of Sioux in the company of General Miles departed for Washington to air their grievances. Joe Ford went with them to market the company's photographs nationally and, according to one report, to sell Big Foot's Ghost Dance shirt.[52] ¶ Ford returned to Chadron on February 12, after spending time in Chicago and Washington, and several days on a snowbound train in the Nebraska Sandhills. Business in the war-view trade was brisk. The partners established a branch studio in Chadron, with half a dozen people hired to print the battlefield scenes. They also had at least three agents besides Joe Ford on the road selling views. It was not until February 20 that Trager, Ford, and Hayword finally filed articles of incorporation. This tardiness in incorporating apparently caused them some subsequent grief, for in June 1891, E. Heyn, an Omaha photographer, filed suit against the partners, demanding a judgment of $283, alleging that they had not complied with the regulations controlling companies in the state.[53] ¶ With the waning of national media attention, and with the military withdrawing, the economy of the area slowly reverted to the depressed levels seen before the troubles began. While news reports indicate that war views were still selling, signs appeared that suggested all was not well. By the end of February the Tragers advertised a special on cabinet card portraits at twelve for $3.50—a far cry from the fifty cents per picture that photographers had received just a month earlier. ¶ Perhaps in desperation, the partners expanded their business to include patent medicine. On March 3, 1891, they traded the relics that they had collected on the battlefield for a half interest in Wilbur Springs, a spring south of Chadron that was a source of mineral water. Claiming the water to be a cure for epilepsy, Trager and Ford promoted it on the back of the photographs sold by the Northwestern Photographic Company. Their advertising tactics changed from promoting war views to selling jewelry and their medicine.[54] ¶ On March 19 Trager went to Rushville, Nebraska, to negotiate the sale of war views with a representative of Buffalo Bill Cody's Wild West show. There is no indication whether or not those negotiations were successful, but given Cody's involvement with the Wounded Knee episode it is likely that some accommodation was reached. Ford continued to travel for the company, though his travels were closer to home, with trips in April limited to Cheyenne and Denver.[55] ¶ By May all of the national preoccupation with the events of November, December, and January evaporated. At the beginning of April, Trager and Ford headed for Wyoming, not to sell photographs, but to prospect in the South Pass region. That week, Ernest Trager went to Crawford to reopen the studio there. George Trager and Joe Ford returned from their Wyoming trip in early August. Trager returned to his Chadron studio, and Ford reopened his auction house and took a job as a night watchman. Later, in November of 1891, he assumed the position of marshal in Chadron.[56] ¶ The winter of 1891–92 sounded the death knell for the Trager photographic studio. Desperate-sounding advertising gimmicks and dramatically reduced prices proved inadequate to support the business, and in June, George Trager announced plans to summer once again in Wyoming. On July 21, 1892, he left for a two-month tour of that state and announced his plans to relocate in Fremont, Nebraska, and go into

Northwestern Photographic Company backprint.

NORTHWESTERN
Photographic Company,
CHADRON,   -   NEBRASKA.

Headquarters for all kinds of Indian and Late War Views of
Pine Ridge Agency, So. Dak.

All Views Copyrighted.

partnership with F. M. Steadman, an established photographer there.[57] ¶ On August 4, 1892, the newspapers announced that Foss and Mossman bought the Tragers' studio and that Ernest Trager would go to work for the Fremont, Elkhorn, and Missouri Valley Railroad in their machine shops at Chadron. George Trager returned in early October of 1892 and tried his hand at the unlikely task of selling eggs. He joined Steadman sometime thereafter. The only evidence for this partnership is a couple of surviving photographs with mounts bearing the name "Trager and Steadman." Steadman himself went out of business on May 1, 1893. After that, all trace of George Trager is lost.[58] ¶ Clarence Moreledge remained at Pine Ridge until at least July 4, 1891, when he photographed the Independence Day celebrations and the peace councils held at that time. His relationship with the Northwestern Photographic Company remained firm, for photographs made at that late date can be found on the company's mounts. ¶ Shortly thereafter he returned to Omaha and established the American Viewing Company. He must have transferred all of his negatives to the Northwestern Photographic Company before he left, for his pictures exist on that company's mounts with his American Viewing Company label rubber-stamped over the Northwestern imprint. Around this same time, Moreledge also established, or at least was associated with, the Southern Photograph Company in Fort Smith, Arkansas. By October 1895 he had moved to Oklahoma City. By 1899 he was back in Fort Smith. In 1900 Moreledge moved to St. Louis, Missouri, where his fortunes turned sour. The *Kansas City Star* of January 22, 1900, reported that Moreledge was involved with a traveling theater company that toured a production of *Faust* to small western towns. The company needed money to continue their tour, and to raise it Moreledge turned to armed robbery. ¶ He held up the McClintock and Lewis Brothers Restaurant on Sunday, January 14, and attempted to repeat his crime the following week. Unfortunately for him, he selected Shattner's Saloon as his second victim where, as luck would have it, George Shearer, a local policeman, was occupying the lavatory. ¶ Moreledge was so quiet in the commission of his crime that Shearer heard nothing, and at first thought that the bartender and customers were joking about the holdup. Once convinced that a crime had occurred, he pursued Moreledge and arrested him. After brief protestations of innocence, Moreledge confessed to both crimes. ¶ Charged with grand larceny, he sat in the county jail for two and a quarter years while the legal system deliberated his case and finally convicted him. Moreledge appealed to the Missouri Supreme Court, but the maximum sentence of five years imposed on him was upheld. To make matters worse, he was given no credit for time served. On April 11, 1902, he was transferred to the Missouri State Penitentiary at Jefferson City to begin his sentence.[59] ¶ The conviction ruined Moreledge, and his physical and mental health deteriorated. On August 2, 1904, Missouri governor A. M. Dockery commuted his sentence, declaring him to be in poor health and of unsound mind. Following his release, Moreledge moved to New York State. After settling in Syracuse, where he may once again have opened a studio, he moved to Sar-atoga Springs, and, finally, to New York City. There he died on July 9, 1948.[60] ¶ Ernest Trager remained in Chadron for a time after the studio closed. In 1893 he married a woman who had worked for him in the studio. Later he and his wife moved to Casper, Wyoming, where he worked for the Standard Oil Company of Indiana. Even though he sold the studio in 1892, it appears that Ernest Trager retained the negatives that he, George Trager, and Clarence Moreledge had made. Thirty-three of the negatives were donated to the Nebraska State Historical Society in 1930 by L. M. Kemp, of Columbus, Nebraska. Kemp found the negatives abandoned in a house formerly occupied by O. E. Trager, who was probably George Trager's son, Otto.[61] ¶ The other negatives remained with Ernest Trager. Mrs. Trager, in a letter to Elmo Scott Watson (a journalist interested in the American West), reported that she had a "fine collection of [Trager's] photographs," which she disposed of after Ernest's death on October 7, 1928. If in fact these were the Northwestern Photographic Company negatives, they disappeared until 1951, when Mrs. Louise Stegner, an Omaha, Nebraska, book dealer sold them to the Denver Public Library, where they are currently held. The works of the other photographers—Grabill, Cross, Butcher, and Meddaugh—have trickled into a number of different institutions and have joined those of Trager and Moreledge as our collective visual memory of the tragedy at Wounded Knee.[62]

The Photographs

Prelude

26. *The Pine Ridge Agency was established in 1879 as the Bureau of Indian Affairs' administrative center for the reservation. In the winter of 1890–91 it also served as a military headquarters during the U.S. Army's occupation of the reservation. This 1891 composite view looks west down the community's main street, which ends at the multistoried Indian boarding school (center background). In front of the school, on the north (right) side of the street, are the agency offices, warehouses, and employees' quarters. The Episcopal church, which served as an Indian hospital after the fighting at Wounded Knee, is at the extreme left.*

P.R. Agency, S. D., looking West. (1891) PEI 134. No 1381.

27, 28, 29, 30. On ration day Indians came to the agency to receive rations of bacon, corn-meal, flour, coffee, and sugar. Up to six hundred women waited patiently in line while the issue agent checked ration cards and doled out the allotted amounts based on the size of the family. The rations were intended to assist the Lakotas while they made the transition from an economy based on buffalo hunting to one of subsistence farming. ¶ In 1890 the rations were reduced about 20 percent. When this reduction combined with a crop failure, the Lakotas undoubtedly did suffer. On November 21, 1890, the Chadron Advocate published Chief Red Cloud's allegation that 217 people had died of starvation at Pine Ridge, but on November 26, 1890, newspaper reporter Carl Smith mentioned in the Omaha World-Herald the "thousands of cattle roaming all over the reservation." Pine Ridge agent H. D. Gallagher had earlier reported that nearly eleven thousand cattle belonging to the Oglalas grazed on the reservation (U.S. Commissioner of Indian Affairs, Fifty-Ninth Annual Report, 1890, 51–52). The Indians did own the cattle, but the agent made all the important decisions about their issuance. The lack of food was often cited as a major cause of the Ghost Dance's popularity. Although privation undoubtedly contributed to the spread of the religion, a more fundamental cause lay in the Lakotas' desire to reclaim control of their own destiny.

31, 32. *A beef issue was described by Dr. Charles A. Eastman, a Pine Ridge Reservation physician:* "Thousands of Indians, scattered over a reservation a hundred miles long by fifty wide, came to the agency for a weekly or fortnightly supply of rations, and it was a veritable 'Wild West' array that greeted my astonished eyes. The streets and stores were alive with a motley crowd in picturesque garb, for all wore their best on these occasions. . . . Toward noon, the whole population moved out two or three miles to a large corral in the midst of a broad prairie, where a herd of beef cattle was held in readiness by the agency cowboys. An Indian with stentorian voice, mounted on a post, announced the names of the group whose steer was to be turned loose. Next moment the flying animal was pursued by two or three swift riders with rifles across their saddles. As the cattle were turned out in quick succession, we soon had a good imitation of the old time buffalo hunt. The galloping, longhorned steers were chased madly in every direction, amid yells and whoops, the firing of guns and clouds of yellow dust, with here and there a puff of smoke and a dull report as one stumbled and fell. The excitement was soon over, and men of each group were busy skinning the animals, dressing the meat and dividing it among the families interested." (Charles A. Eastman, *From the Deep Woods to Civilization*, 79–80.).

33. Though identified as a Scalp Dance by the photographer, the dance portrayed in this image is probably an Omaha Dance. The Bureau of Indian Affairs banned many Indian ceremonies, including the Ghost Dance becauses of its Indian religious content and the Scalp Dance because of its militaristic content. This performance is in front of Dr. Charles A. Eastman's medical office. A drawing of this photo appeared in the Omaha Weekly World-Herald on January 28, 1891, as an "Omaha Dance at the Agency."

34. Daniel F. Royer (center), an Alpena, South Dakota, physician, was a spoils-system appointee to the position of agent on the Pine Ridge Reservation. Arriving in late September 1890, his paramount concern was the suppression of the Ghost Dance. It was soon evident that he was not the man for the job. In a letter of October 12 to Thomas J. Morgan, the commissioner of Indian affairs, he wrote, "I have been carefully investigating the matter [of the Ghost Dance] and I find I have an elephant on my hands." (Letter . . . relative to . . . Indians in certain States, 51st Cong., 2nd sess., 1891, Senate Ex. Doc. No.9, 5.) By the end of the month he was insisting that military intervention on the reservation was necessary not only to suppress the new religion but to protect whites from an outbreak. A war, he thought, was inevitable.

35. An Indian police force was established on the Pine Ridge Reservation in 1879 and performed effectively when dealing with routine matters, but was unable to enforce the Bureau of Indian Affairs' ban on the Ghost Dance. The Pine Ridge police were first ordered to halt a ceremony at White Bird's camp in July 1890. They were outnumbered by camp guards armed with Winchester rifles and were forced to retreat. The police were not issued rifles until near the end of the year. ¶ George Sword (left foreground) was the Pine Ridge police chief. Previous to this time he had participated in the Sun Dance and fought against the U. S. Army to perserve the Lakotas' old way of life, but he had come to believe that the white man's way was the only means of survival.

36. Black Dog posed for this George Trager portrait. By the time of this photograph the police had been armed with Springfields, to go along with their Remington pistols.

37. *George Bartlett, as deputy U.S. marshal for the Pine Ridge and Rosebud reservations, represented another arm of federal authority. His job usually involved enforcing federal laws as they related to whites living on Indian lands rather than apprehending Sioux suspects. Bartlett, here with an Indian police family at Pine Ridge, was sent by Brigadier General John R. Brooke in early December to No Water's camp to persuade him to stop Ghost Dancing. Together with inducements of food and protection, councils such as this brought several groups of Indians to the agency, where they acknowledged the authority of the government.*

38. *Although only about one-third of the Lakotas became Ghost Dancers, many others, like Red Cloud, gave their tacit support. The aging but still influential Oglala chief denied any connection with the religion, but Agent Royer's assessment of the chief's position was probably more accurate. In an October 30, 1890 letter, he wrote, "While Red Cloud is not a prominent man in the dance, he is quietly encouraging his people to keep it going."* (Royer to R. V. Belt, Letter . . . relative to . . . Indians in certain States, 51st Cong., 2nd sess., 1891, Senate Ex. Doc. No.9, 10.) *Red Cloud did write a letter to Big Foot urging the Miniconjou to come to Pine Ridge. According to Dewey Beard, the letter contributed to the band's decision to leave their homes on a journey that would end at Wounded Knee Creek.* (Donald F. Danker, "The Wounded Knee Interviews of Eli S. Ricker," 180.)

Chief Red Clouds Home
Pine Ridge S.D.

39. Red Cloud stands in front of his home, an agency landmark, which was described by Emma Sickels, a Pine Ridge teacher: "Across from the boarding-school of the Pine Ridge Agency, on the opposite ridge, separated by the hollow of the creek, is a two-story frame house, surrounded by some desolate-looking tepees, a few log buildings and sweat-houses. Wagons and woodpiles complete the settlement. This is Red Cloud's camp, and the largest house in his residence--the only two-story dwelling at the agency. It was built for Red Cloud to distinguish him from the others of his band." (W. Fletcher Johnson, *Life of Sitting Bull and the History of the Indian War,* 369.) ¶ The Bureau of Indian Affairs built the house in 1879 at a cost of five hundred dollars as part of its program to "civilize" the Oglalas. Bureau officials hoped other Indians would follow the chief's example and abandon their tipis in favor of frame or log homes. By 1890 most families had built log houses, but they continued to spend much of their time in nearby tipis.

40. On November 11, 1890, Agent Royer issued a warrant for the arrest of Little. Royer explained: "Today I ordered the second lieutenant [Thunder Bear] of [the] police force to arrest an Indian that had violated the law in several instances, one of the charges being that he has been killing cattle promiscuously over the reservation. On being informed by the police that I wished him brought to the office, he drew his knife and positively refused to be arrested, and a mob of the ghost dancers rushed in and relieved their fellow dancer from the hands of the police, taking him away to their camps, and boasting of their power and making all kinds of fun over the attempted arrest and the inefficiency of the police force, etc." ¶ The incident fueled Royer's fears. He wrote, "We have no protection and are at the mercy of these crazy dancers." Agents on other reservations and civilians had been expressing similar concerns. When Royer stepped up his dire warnings of impending trouble, the commissioner of Indian affairs decided it was time to request military assistance. (Royer to Morgan, Nov. 11 and 13, 1890, Letter . . . relative to . . . Indians in certain States, 51st Cong., 2nd sess., 1891, Senate Ex. Doc. No.9, 16 and 19.)

41. *Jack Red Cloud, son of the famous chief, was an early convert to the Ghost Dance religion but later worked for a peaceful settlement to the problems besetting the believers. He was among the Ghost Dancers who prevented Agent Royer's police from arresting Little. At the height of this confrontation the Sioux chief American Horse stepped forward to urge restraint on the part of the believers. Jack Red Cloud drew his pistol and threatened American Horse, asserting that such a conciliatory attitude was a cause of many of their problems. Fortunately the tense moment passed. But in the weeks that followed, Jack Red Cloud accompanied Father John Jutz, a Catholic missionary, to the Stronghold to persuade the militant believers to surrender. After the Wounded Knee fighting, he retreated to the Stronghold, as did most believers, but was among the first group to open discussions for a surrender. ¶ The younger Red Cloud posed a difficult question to opponents of the Ghost Dance. In an interview published in the* Omaha World-Herald *on November 23, 1890, he said, "White men had religions and religious celebrations. Why shouldn't an Indian be treated just the same?"*

Jack Red Cloud

42. *American Horse was a staunch supporter of the Indian Bureau's policies. He was present when the police tried to arrest Little. Elaine Goodale Eastman was there and described the scene: "At this juncture a progressive chief named American Horse appeared unarmed in the doorway, quelled the tumult with a few plain words, telling them that they could easily kill a policeman or two, but that in the end both they and their families would be wiped out by avenging troops. Very possibly he saved all our lives."* (Elaine Goodale Eastman, *Sister to the Sioux . . . 1885–91,* 146.)

43. *Agent Royer (the eighth standing person from the right) made a desperate plea for troops on Thursday, November 13, 1890. One week later they came. This gathering of soldiers and civilians is captured by photographer Clarence Grant Moreledge, poised by the cannon's wheel, with his hand on a shutter release bulb.* ¶ *General Brooke arrived at the agency with his troops and took charge. Brooke's first job was quickly accomplished— to restore order and federal authority at the agency. His second job was more complicated and required more time and more troops—to restore order on the entire reservation. He adopted a policy developed by Major General Nelson A. Miles of "coaxing" as many of the disenchanted Sioux to the agency with a combination of promises and threats. He promised them food and redresses for wrongs and threatened military retaliation if the Ghost Dancers left their reservations. Although progress appeared agonizingly slow to civilian observers, Brooke's efforts seemed to work.*

View of Battery at
Pine Ridge Agency
210,

44. *The Second United States Infantry set up camp at Pine Ridge Agency. Brooke's initial force consisted of four companies of the Second Infantry from Fort Omaha, three troops of the Ninth Cavalry, and one company of the Eighth Infantry from Fort Robinson. Setting up their Sibley tents, not the warmest quarters for winter duty, the infantry guarded the agency. The cavalry scouted the surrounding land.*

45. *Although the months of November and December proved to be unseasonably warm, the Second Infantry prepared for the winter. A steady stream of supplies poured from the railroad station at Rushville to the Pine Ridge Agency. A letter from a sister camp at Rosebud Agency described the soldiers' unenviable lot: "The chilly November nights already give us a fair taste of what a winter campaign under canvas is like in this climate, and our only* consolation is that the noble red man is probably as uncomfortable in his tepee as we are in a wall tent." ("Our Special Reports from the Indian Country," Army and Navy Journal, Dec. 6, 1890.) ¶ The presence of so many soldiers meant boom times for the area's merchants and freighters. The neighboring town of Chadron, Nebraska, even sent a delegation of businessmen to General Brooke to encourage him to throw some of the business to them.

46. One company of the Eighth U.S. Infantry, commanded by Captain Augustus W. Corliss, acted as artillery with a complement of Hotchkiss and Gatling guns. Besides setting up residence, the army's activities during its first week included securing the road and repairing the telegraph line between Rushville and Pine Ridge. Any sort of violence between the soldiers and the Indians was scrupulously avoided. Good intentions aside, the presence of over four hundred troops did little to ease the minds of the Sioux, two thousand of whom were camped across White Clay Creek to the west. ¶ The arrival of troops on the adjoining Rosebud Reservation prompted an exodus of most of the Brules to Pine Ridge. As tensions cooled on the Rosebud reservation, they rose at Pine Ridge. Peaceful meals at the agency belied its being within the eye of a hurricane.

47. *Civilians, scouts, and soldiers congregate on Pine Ridge's main street. Henry Dawson's store is at the extreme right.*

48. *A crowd in front of Dawson's store included photographer Clarence Grant Moreledge, the tall, clean-shaven young man on the steps.*

Birds Eeye View Of
7th Cav Camp at the late
Indian War & Pine Ridge Ag. S.D. Nov 27th
From Fort Riley Kas

49. Top left: The Seventh U.S. Cavalry left Fort Riley, Kansas, on November 23, debarked at Rushville (pictured here) on the morning of the twenty-sixth, and left the same day for Pine Ridge. A news dispatch from Rushville asserted, "After viewing the arrival of the soldiers during the past few days the last vestige of fear of the Indians has apparently departed from the settlers of this vicinity and it is believed that the impression made on the redskins will be equally subduing." (Omaha Bee, Nov. 27, 1891, dateline Nov. 26.)

50. Bottom left: The Seventh Cavalry arrived at Pine Ridge after a twenty-five-mile ride from Rushville. No other cavalry regiment in the entire army evoked the images of the old Indian-fighting army than it did. Several of its officers and men had fought at the Little Big Horn, and, because of this and romantic notions of fate and destiny, the myth of a "revenge" motive for its actions at Wounded Knee gained undue credibility. Evening the score for Custer was probably far removed from the minds of the dozens of raw recruits who peppered the ranks. Lieutenant John C.

Gresham, Troop I of the Seventh, wrote that before their arrival, "Eighty-five per cent of our men had seen nothing of Indians—indeed, had no knowledge of them beyond what is usually acquired at home by city or country boys of their class and station." (John C. Gresham, "The Story of Wounded Knee.") The fame of the Seventh Cavalry, though, ensured the marketability of its photographs. This scene reappeared in later printings, with an updated but vague label, "7th Cav. camp before the fight, Dec. 29," doubtless to make it more timely

and hence salable. The man in the foreground is not a sentry but rather the photographer Moreledge.

51. Above: After the army occupied the Pine Ridge Reservation, General Brooke ordered the Indians to abandon their homes and Ghost Dance camps and move to the agency. He hoped to separate the "friendly" from the "hostile" Indians so he could deal with the latter more effectively. Big Road and Little Wound were among the Ghost Dance leaders who chose to move to the agency.

52. *Although Big Road dressed in "citizen's clothing" for this portrait, his acceptance of the trappings of the white world was slow and probably painful. In the early part of November he and Good Thunder organized a Ghost Dance at the mouth of Wounded Knee Creek. When the army occupied the reservations, Big Road and his Oglala followers grudgingly obeyed the order to move to the agency. After fighting broke out at Wounded Knee Creek, the band fled to the Stronghold. Finding themselves surrounded by an overwhelming and threatening military force, Big Road, Jack Red Cloud, and a few others returned to the agency to discuss the terms of a surrender.*

53. *Lieutenant Edward W. Casey (center foreground), Twenty-second U.S. Infantry, recruited this troop of about fifty Cheyenne scouts at the Tongue River Reservation in Montana. Their agent had reported, "The Cheyenne are very anxious to fight the Sioux as they have an old grudge against them."* (John Tully to the Commissioner of Indian Affairs, Dec. 1, 1890, Reports and Correspondence Relating to the Army Investigations of the Battle of Wounded Knee and to the Sioux Campaign of 1890–91, National Archives Microfilm Publication M983.) ¶ *The scouts left Fort Keogh for Pine Ridge on November 27. Near the end of December, they were assigned to Lieutenant Colonel George B. Sanford's Ninth Cavalry and were patrolling the perimeter of the Stronghold to prevent the escape of the Ghost Dancers. Lieutenant Robert N. Getty (left center, in kepi hat) assumed command after Casey's death in January.*

54, 55. *Over one hundred members of the infant Hospital Corps served during the Sioux campaign. The peaceful days of late November and early December allowed time for field training. Exercises involved giving first aid, moving the wounded, and managing field hospitals. Corpsmen were assigned to each regiment. At Wounded Knee, one steward was killed and two privates in the Hospital Corps rescued an officer, for which they later received certificates of merit.*

56, 57. Elaine Goodale Eastman described the situation at the Pine Ridge Indian school during the winter of 1890–91: "The doors of the large Oglala boarding school were kept locked by day as well as by night and the grounds, surrounded by a high fence of barbed wire, constantly patrolled by armed guards. These boys and girls, held partly as hostages for the good behavior of their parents, in part for their own protection, must be fed, taught, and kept in order." (Elaine Goodale Eastman, Sister to the Sioux . . . 1885–91, 156.) ¶ The school was opened in 1884 and soon enlarged to accommodate 200 children. In 1890 the average daily attendance was 166. Children might be kept at the school for weeks or even months while they were rigorously trained in proper white manners and customs as well as academic subjects. The building was destroyed by fire in February 1894.

58. Three rural day schools for Indian students were burned and teachers and other school employees were ordered to the safety of the agency in early December. One schoolteacher, Thisba Hutson Morgan (fifth from the left, standing), remembered when the news of Wounded Knee reached the school: "It was the noon hour and the children were scattered over the grounds at work and at play, awaiting their call to dinner, when the first runners from the battlefield reached the Agency. The children were the first to get the news and report it to us, because they could interpret the sign language of the runners as they reached the knoll behind the school house, outstripping the Army couriers, swift though they were. The children were panic stricken as more news came in for many of them knew that their parents must have been in the fray. A few of them escaped in their excitement. . . . We hurried them into the house, battening the doors and windows, and each of the twenty or more teachers stood guard in turn while the others tried to sooth and comfort the best we could the wailing, hysterical, fainting children who could hear those coming from the battlefield call to them to get away for they were going to shoot fire-arrows into the roof of the school house and burn it. The teachers soon sensed that their safety depended upon keeping the children in the school house." (Thisba Hutson Morgan, "Reminiscences . . . of the Ogllala Sioux," 24, 54, 56.)

59. Standing Rock Reservation, the home of Sitting Bull, suffered its own problems. Although not a hereditary chief, Sitting Bull had a loyal following among the Hunkpapas. He had a well-deserved reputation for his tenacious adherence to the traditional Lakota lifestyle and engaged in a decade-long contest of wills over reservation policy with Agent James McLaughlin. After a visit from Kicking Bear in October of 1890, Sitting Bull's people embraced the Ghost Dance. The agent seized this opportunity to deprive Sitting Bull of his political power. On December 15 the agency police were sent to arrest Sitting Bull, who resisted. A fight broke out, in which fourteen Indians were killed, including the Hunkpapa leader.

60. The Standing Rock Agency police who were killed during Sitting Bull's attempted arrest on December 15 were buried two days later in this civilian cemetery near the agency. Sitting Bull's remains were interred at the nearby Fort Yates military cemetery. The dead Ghost Dancers were buried a few days later by the missionary Thomas L. Riggs in a mass grave near Sitting Bull's home. ¶ The survivors, fearing retribution, fled the reservation. Within the next ten days nearly 230 were captured by Colonel Henry C. Merriam's Seventh Infantry, which had been patrolling along the Cheyenne River. They were imprisoned briefly at Fort Sully and then returned to their homes. About forty persons joined Big Foot's band and some of those were killed at Wounded Knee.

Fort Yates,

Geo. W. Scott,

N. Dakota.

61. George W. Scott, a Fort Yates photographer, wasted no time in staging a reenactment of Sitting Bull's arrest for the camera. Others dismantled Sitting Bull's cabin and shipped it to Chicago, where it was rebuilt and displayed during the Columbian Exposition of 1892.

62. Lieutenant Colonel Edwin V. Sumner, Eighth Cavalry, took command of Camp Cheyenne in early December. From this camp his troopers, one of whom is shown here, kept watch on Big Foot's band. Hunkpapa refugees from the Sitting Bull fight joined the Miniconjous at the same time Sumner received an arrest order for Big Foot. When Big Foot and his followers gave Sumner the slip on December 23 and began their trek to Pine Ridge Reservation, it set in motion events that would culminate in the bloodshed at Wounded Knee.

"The Opening of the Fight at Wounded Knee." (Harper's Weekly, Jan. 24, 1891.) The noted western artist Frederic Remington depended on the accounts of Seventh cavalrymen for his 1891 drawing. Neither he nor any photographer witnessed the events at Wounded Knee. Photographers recorded the carnage five days later. ¶ Philip F. Wells, a mixed-blood Sioux and one of the few eyewitnesses to the Wounded Knee fight who was fluent in both Lakota and English, recounted the events of that Monday morning: "I was interpreting for General Forsyth just before the battle of Wounded Knee, December 29, 1890. The captured Indians had been ordered to give up their arms, but Big Foot replied that his people had no arms. Forsyth said to me, 'Tell Big Foot he says the Indians have no arms, yet yesterday they were well armed when they surrendered. He is deceiving me. Tell him he need have no fear in giving up his arms, as I wish to treat him kindly.' Continuing, Forsyth said, 'Have I not done enough to convince you that I intend nothing but kindness? Did I not put you into an ambulance and have my doctors care for you? Did I not put you in a good tent with a stove to keep you warm and comfortable? I have sent for provisions, which I expect soon, so I can feed your people.'

"Big Foot replied, 'They have no guns, except such as you have found. I collected all my guns at the Cheyenne River Agency and turned them in. They were all burned.'

"They had about a dozen old-fashioned guns, tied together with strings—not a decent one in the lot.

"Forsyth declared, 'You are lying to me in return for my kindness.'

"While the soldiers were searching for arms, Big Foot gave substantially the same answer as before.

"During this time a medicine man, gaudily dressed and fantastically painted, executed the maneuvers of the ghost dance, raising and throwing dust into the air. He exclaimed, 'Ha! Ha!' as he did so, meaning he was about to do something terrible, and said, 'I have lived long enough,' meaning he would fight until he died.

"Turning to the young warriors, who were squatted together, he said, 'Do not fear, but let your hearts be strong. Many soldiers are about us and have many bullets, but I am assured their bullets cannot penetrate us. The prairie is large, and their bullets will fly over the prairies and will not come toward us. If they do come toward us, they will float away like dust in the air.'

"Then the young warriors exclaimed, 'How!' with great earnestness, meaning they would back the medicine man.

"I turned to Major Whitside and said, 'That man is making mischief,' and repeated what he had said.

"Whitside replied, 'Go direct to Colonel Forsyth and tell him about it,' which I did.

"Forsyth and I went to the circle of warriors, where he told me to tell the medicine man, who was engaged in silent maneuvers and incantations, to sit down and keep quiet, but he paid no attention to the order. Forsyth repeated the order. After I had translated it into the Indian language, Big Foot's brother-in-law answered, 'He will sit down when he gets around the circle.'

"When the medicine man came to the end of the circle, he squatted down.

"Big Foot's brother-in-law asked at the end of the conversation that the Indians be permitted to take Big Foot, who he said was dying, and continue the journey begun before the troops intercepted them.

"Forsyth replied, 'I can take better care of him here than you can elsewhere, as I will have my doctors attend him.'

"Forsyth then went to one side to give instructions elsewhere. A cavalry sergeant exclaimed, 'There goes an Indian with a gun under his blanket!' Forsyth ordered him to take the gun from the Indian, which he did.

"Whitside then said to me, 'Tell the Indians it is necessary that they be searched one at a time.'

"The old Indians assented willingly by answering, 'How!' and the search began.

"The young warriors paid no attention to what I told them, but the old men—five or six of them—sitting next to us, passed through the lines and submitted to search. All this time I kept watching the medicine man, who was doing the ghost dance, for fear he might cause trouble. While turning my eyes momentarily away, I heard some one on my left exclaim, 'Look out! Look out!' Turning my head and bringing my arms to 'port,' I saw five or six young warriors cast off their blankets and pull guns out from under them and brandish them in the air. One of the warriors shot into the soldiers, who were ordered to fire into the Indians. The older Indians sitting between the younger ones and us immediately rose up so that the farther end of the circle, forty or fifty feet away, was hidden from my view. I heard a shot from the midst of the Indians. As I started to cock my rifle, I looked in the direction of the medicine man. He or some other medicine man approached to within three or four feet of me with a long cheese knife, ground to a sharp point and raised to stab me. The fight between us prevented my seeing anything else at the time. He stabbed me during the melee and nearly cut off my nose. I held him off until I could swing my rifle to hit him, which I did. I shot and killed him in self-defence and as an act of war as soon as I could gain room to aim my rifle and fire.

"By the time a general fight was raging between the soldiers and the Indians. Troop 'K' was drawn up between the tents of the women and children and the main body of the Indians, who had been summoned to deliver their arms. The Indians began firing into 'Troop K' to gain the canyon of Wounded Knee creek. In doing so they exposed their women and children to their own fire. Captain Wallace was killed at this time while standing in front of his troops. A bullet, striking him in the forehead, plowed away the top of his head. I started to pull off my nose, which hung by the skin, but Lieutenant Guy Preston shouted, 'My God, Man! Don't do that! That can be saved!' He then led me away from the scene of the trouble." (Philip F. Wells, "Ninety-six Years among the Indians of the Northwest," 285–87.)

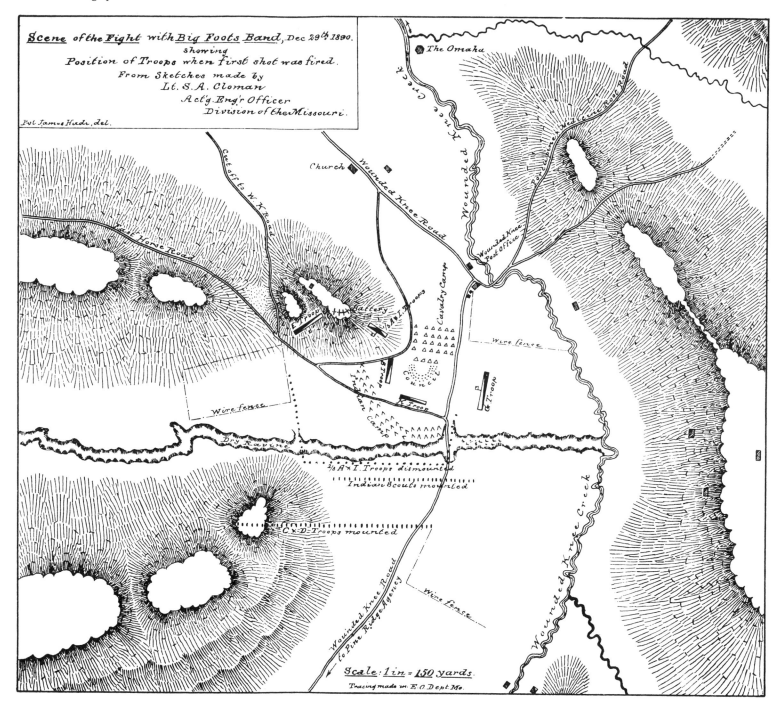

The Battlefield

63. This Trager view to the west across Wounded Knee Creek is similar to the scene described by Private August Hettinger, who arrived a few days after the fight: "We crossed the brow of a small hill and beheld a small valley, about one-half mile wide, spread out in front [west] of us, a small creek fringed with brush and cottonwoods meandered down through the center and finally disappeared to the northwest in some pine covered rough hills. This was our first sight of Wounded Knee creek. . . . We could see on the other side of the creek the ground strewn with the bodies of horses and even wagons, and the remnants of a burned camp and what looked like the bodies of human beings could be seen over an area of 200 or 300 acres." (August Hettinger, "Personal Recollections of the 'Messiah Craze Campaign.' ") ¶ Hettinger was on a forced march from the Rosebud Agency under the command of Captain Folliot A. Whitney, Eighth Infantry. Apparently they had been sent out to meet a second contingent from Pine Ridge, which included a civilian burial party. The burial detail, delayed due to a concern about a possible Indian attack, arrived with a military escort on January 3, 1891, and began its task of interring the dead. ¶ The burial party is barely visible in the distance to the left of and slightly beyond the large trees.

64. This view is to the southeast from the hill where the Indian dead were interred. The tipi poles at the right mark the location of the Indian camp. The army camp was at the extreme left. At the center, where men are loading the frozen bodies into a wagon, was the council circle where Colonel Forsyth ordered the Indians to surrender their arms. A second photographer stands to the left, with his camera.

65. *Members of the burial party, including an Indian woman, examine the western edge of the Indian camp. The mass grave is being dug on the hill at the left, where the Hotchkiss guns had been placed. The view is to the northwest. The Northwestern Photographic Company copyrighted its photographs effective January 1 although, according to the Omaha Bee and Captain Frank D. Baldwin's report, they must have been shot on January 3 (Omaha Bee, Jan. 4, 1891, dateline Jan. 3, and Baldwin to the Assistant Adjutant General, Jan. 5, 1891,* Army Investigations of Wounded Knee, *1075–76.)*

66. *Reporter Charles W. Allen witnessed the fighting at Wounded Knee. He would recall:* "We rode past what but recently had been the site of a far-flung camp of white and brown army tents and the grimy old canvas of torn tepees; now marked only, here and there, by the bended willow frames and shattered poles of what so lately were shelters for the living." (Charles W. Allen, "In the West That Was: Memoirs, Sketches, and Legends," MS2635, 285, Nebraska State Historical Society.)

67. The burial detail works near the center of the Indian camp. Captain Whitney counted only forty-seven dead in the camp, but noted: "There is evidence that a greater number of bodies have been removed. Since the snow, wagon tracks were made near where it is supposed dead or wounded Indians had been lying." (Whitney to the Assistant Adjutant General, Jan. 3, 1891, *Army Investigations of Wounded Knee*, 284.) *An Indian rescue party from the agency had gone to Wounded Knee on January 1 and found several survivors (Omaha Bee, Jan. 2, 1891 [dateline Jan. 1], and Jan. 14, 1891.) The rescuers were forced to abandon their mission when they were fired on by other Indians who misunderstood their intentions. The view is to the northeast, across the Indian camp.*

68. *The shattered wagon near the center of this view might be the one described by Peter McFarland, a government drayman present at the fight:* "The Hotchkiss guns on the hill fired into an Indian wagon. . . . Several Indians were firing on the soldiers from behind this wagon. The shell sent into it knocked it to pieces and killed a number of warriors." (Peter McFarland interview, MS 8, tablet 31, page 95, Ricker Collection, Nebraska State Historical Society.) *The view is from the center of the Indian camp to the northeast, across the council circle.*

69. The man standing in front of the horse and rider holds moccasins and other souvenirs of the massacre. George H. Harries, a Washington correspondent, visited the battleground three weeks later and wrote: "The relic hunter has been all over the battlefield and has taken away everything of value and interest that was above the surface. Occasionally one will find a memento worth carrying away but not often. Whatever was beautiful or odd in the clothing of dead or wounded Indians was taken by the victors and either kept for personal gratification or sold for cash." (*Washington (D.C.) Evening Star*, Jan. 26, 1891.) The view is to the south-west, from the center of the council circle.

70. Charles W. Allen, one of the three newspaper correspondents present at the Wounded Knee fight, recalled the scene in the council circle: "The first gun had no sooner been fired than it was followed by hundreds of others and the battle was on. The fighting continued for about half an hour, and then was continued in skirmish for another hour. When the smoke cleared away from in front of the tent where it began, there were forty-five dead Indians with their impregnable ghost shirts on laying dead on a space of ground about two hundred yards in diameter." (*Chadron (Nebraska) Democrat*, Jan. 1, 1891.)

Birds Eye View of Battle Field at
Wounded Knee S.D.
Copy Righted Jan 1 st 1891 by the
North Western Phot. Co Chadron Neb

71. Reporter Carl Smith was with the burial party when he described a medicine man: "In one square of less than half an acre there were forty-eight bodies stiffened by the frost. Near the center of this collection was what would be taken for a nucleus formed by the fall of four men together. One had a face which was hideous to view. . . . He had originally fallen on his face, and he must have lain in that position for some time, as it was flattened on one side. His hands were clenched, his teeth were clenched, and his body seemed to have a tense appearance. One hand was raised in the air. The arm had frozen in that position." (Chicago Inter-Ocean, Jan. 7, 1891.) ¶ The negative from which its companion was printed was retouched so as to not offend Victorian sensibilities. The rifle was undoubtedly placed at the side of the corpse to enhance the effect. The view is to the east, across the south edge of the council circle.

72. A medicine man played a pivotal role in the tragedy at Wounded Knee. He was performing the Ghost Dance and threw a handful of dirt in the air. The first gunshot of the fight rang out almost immediately thereafter. Some of the army officers later asserted that the dirt throwing was a prearranged signal to begin fighting, but most of the witnesses rejected that assumption. ¶ Ethnologist James Mooney's often-repeated identification of the medicine man as Yellow Bird cannot be substantiated. Four eyewitnesses, three Miniconjous and one mixed-blood, identified him as Sits Straight, also called Good Thunder. (Wells, "Ninety-six years . . . ," statement of Elk Saw Him, 293; B. J. Peterson, The Battle of Wounded Knee, statement of Philip Wells, 19; Washington (D.C.) Evening Star, Jan. 28 and 30, 1891, statement of Long Bull; and Donald F. Danker, "The Wounded Knee Interviews of Eli S. Ricker," statement of Joseph Horn Cloud, 173.) There is no mention of a Yellow Bird at Wounded Knee in any of the accounts of the day. ¶ The identity of the central figure in this image is not known. Joseph Horn Cloud mentioned another man, Shakes Bird, who was also singing Ghost songs when the fighting started. He was killed and perhaps is the man in this photograph.

73. *Big Foot was only wounded in the initial burst of gunfire and was killed later in the morning when his movements attracted the attention of the soldiers, according to Charles Allen* (Charles W. Allen, "In the West That Was . . . ," MS 2635, 279, Nebraska State Historical Society). *He had contracted pneumonia, and the night before the battle Major Whitside had insisted that he sleep in an army tent equipped with a stove, which may be the one in the background of this photograph. On the morning of December 29, he was moved to the nearby council circle.*

74. Reporter Carl Smith described the dead Miniconjou leader in the Chicago Inter-Ocean on January 7, 1891: "Big Foot lay in a sort of solitary dignity. . . . He was dressed in fairly good civilian clothing, his head being tied up in a scarf. He had underwear of wool and his general appearance was that of a fairly prosperous personage. He was shot through and through, and if he ever knew what hurt him, appearances dissembled very much. A wandering photographer propped the old man up, and as he lay there defenseless his portrait was taken. . . . He was however spared the customary adjuration to look pleasant."

75. Lieutenant Sydney A. Cloman, First
Infantry, surveys the carnage from the north
edge of the council circle. He accompanied the
burial party and drew the army's official map
of the scene of the fighting. Chief Big Foot's
body also lies to the left. The view is to the
northeast.

76. The burial party collected the dead from the ravine south of the Indian camp where many had sought shelter. Army officers look on.

77. Dewey Beard, a Miniconjou, took refuge in the ravine and later described some of the action that took place there: "I was badly wounded and pretty weak too. While I was lying on my back, I looked down the ravine and saw a lot of women coming up and crying. When I saw these women, girls and little girls and boys coming up, I saw soldiers on both sides of the ravine shoot at them until they had killed every one of them." Later he saw a young woman who "was crying and calling 'Mother! Mother!' She was wounded under her chin, close to her throat, and the bullet had passed through a braid of her hair and carried some of it into the wound. . . . Her mother had been shot down behind her." (Donald F. Danker, "The Wounded Knee Interviews of Eli S. Ricker," 195.)

78. One hundred forty-six bodies were interred in a mass grave on the small hill where the Hotchkiss guns had been positioned.

Burial of the Dead
at the Battle of Wounded Knee, S.D.
Copy Righted Jan 31 1891 by the
North Western Photo Co
Chadron Neb
No 1

The War's End

79. *After the first reports of the Wounded Knee massacre came in, the Indians camped around the agency panicked, struck their tipis, and stampeded north. Many Sioux men became enraged and fired on the soldiers' camp from long range. Brooke ordered his men to hold their fire. Civilians were convinced that the agency would be attacked, but it never happened. ¶ Although a photographer described this view as having been taken at the moment of the Indians' shooting, an engraving of it appeared in the* Omaha Weekly World-Herald *on January 28, 1891, labeled "United States soldiers watching the Indians." The photograph smacks of a staged scene. Troops crouched on the right appear ready for action; the men to the far left appear too nonchalant to be actually under fire.*

80, 81. *Although over two dozen reporters vied for Pine Ridge news, the local talent scooped the eastern war correspondents on the* Wounded Knee *story. Eyewitness accounts were written by Charles W. Allen, editor of the* Chadron Democrat *and also on the* New York Herald *payroll; C. H. Cressey,* Omaha Bee; *and William F. Kelley,* Nebraska State Journal (Lincoln). *Allen, who was with Little Bat Garnier and a firearm search party when the shooting started, barely avoided being shot by excited soldiers. Cressey was standing next to Colonel Forsyth. Kelley took up the rifle of a fallen soldier and joined the fight. Kelley also won the honor of having his story filed first. ¶ Left to right, Cressey; Kelley; Major John M. Burke, general manager of Buffalo Bill's* Wild West *show; an unidentified Indian man; Professor Gilbert E. Bailey,* Chicago Inter-Ocean; *Alfred Burkholder,* New York Herald *and* Chamberlain (South Dakota) Gazette; *and Allen.*

82. *The first news stories of the killings at Wounded Knee were written in the small log cabin shown here, just behind the Wounded Knee post office. As Allen, Cressey, and Kelley wrote their copy, occasional gunshots could still be heard. The small cabin was the home of Louis Mousseau, a French mixed-blood, who operated the combination post office and store. This was the nucleus of a small community. There was a day school, a little-used Presbyterian church, and a nearby dance lodge. George Bartlett (standing) had a financial interest in the store.*

7ᵗʰ Cav Coming into Camp from
Wounded Knee Fight with Big Foots Band
Pine Ridge Agcy S.D.

83. The Seventh Cavalry left Wounded Knee for Pine Ridge Agency. One cavalryman later wrote, "Slowly, for the sake of the wounded, the long column left the battleground where the reds were lying as dark spots in the winter night and their sign of peace, the white flag, was moving gently with the wind." (Reminiscence of Ragnar Theodore Ling-Vannerus [Theodore Ragnar at his enlistment] from Christer Lindberg's "Foreigners in Action at Wounded Knee.") ¶ This view was probably photographed on November 27, 1890, and updated by the photographer when he learned of the Seventh Cavalry's role. The column returned to the agency long after nightfall, making this scene impossible to capture on film with the cameras then available.

84. *Before the* Wounded Knee *tragedy, members of Troop B, Seventh Cavalry, posed for a group portrait. This was probably taken at their camp on November 27.*

85. *After the fighting at* Wounded Knee, *a decimated troop posed once again. B Troop had been in a line between the council circle and the ravine. The entire regiment's dead from the* Wounded Knee *disaster numbered thirty. Those whose bodies were unclaimed, along with High Back Bone, a government scout killed during the fight, were buried in the agency cemetery.*

86. Corporal Paul H. Weinert won the Medal of Honor because of his role at Wounded Knee, as did twenty-seven others for their exploits during the entire campaign. His particular instrument of death was the Hotchkiss gun, a breech-loading cannon that fired an explosive shell measuring 3.2 inches. Four such artillery pieces (but no Gatling guns, contrary to some stories) accompanied the Seventh Cavalry. Weinert took the place of his fallen commander and fired the piece with devastating effect. As the fighting progressed, he rolled the gun down the hill to the ravine. "They kept yelling at me to come back, and I kept yelling for a cool gun—there were three more on the hill not in use. Bullets were coming like hail from the Indians' Winchesters. The wheels of my gun were bored full of holes and our clothing was marked in several places. Once a cartridge was knocked out of my hand just as I was about to put it in the gun, and it's a wonder the cartridge didn't explode. I kept going in farther, and pretty soon everything was quiet at the other end of the line." (W. F. Beyer and O. F. Keydel, eds., Deeds of Valor, 2:316.)

87. Before the fighting at Wounded Knee, Lieutenant Colonel Dallas Bache, medical director of the Department of the Platte, had shipped tents and equipment to Pine Ridge for a hospital of twenty-five beds. As more troops arrived, he increased the capacity to sixty. The hospital was staffed with a surgeon, an assistant surgeon, two noncommissioned officers, and ten privates of the Hospital Corps. Wounded soldiers arrived here at 9:30 P.M., December 29.

88. The Holy Cross Episcopal Church at Pine Ridge served as a hospital for some of the Indian survivors brought back from *Wounded Knee* by the U. S. Army. Elaine Goodale Eastman described the scene there: "pews were torn from their fastenings and armfuls of hay fetched by Indian helpers. Upon a layer of this we spread quilts and blankets taken from our own beds. The victims were lifted as gently as possible [from the army wagons] and laid in two long rows on the floor—a pitiful array of young girls and women and babes in arms, little children, and a few men, all pierced with bullets." *A Christmas tree had been removed, but the "joyous green garlands still wreathed windows and doors."* (Elaine Goodale Eastman, Sister to the Sioux, . . . 1885–91, 161–62.)

89. At least thirty-six wounded Indians were treated at the Episcopal church. Susette LaFlesche Tibbles, the wife of Thomas Tibbles, a correspondent for the Omaha World-Herald, talked to one of them, a "young girl, who had a ghost shirt on underneath her clothes [who] said, 'They told me if I put this on the bullets would not go through, and I believed them. Now see where we are.'" Mrs. Tibbles comforted another victim, describing his plight: "There was a little boy with his throat apparently shot to pieces. . . . When I saw him yesterday afternoon he looked worse than the day before and when they feed him now the food and water come out of the side of his neck." (Omaha World-Herald, Jan. 2, 1891.) ¶ The injury was examined by Captain and Assistant Surgeon Francis Joseph Ives, who identified the five-year-old child as Steals a Running Horse. He also treated the wife of Big Foot. Her cot was in the chancel (extreme left). She had two flesh wounds, which became infected; she then contracted pneumonia and died on January 13. (Frank J. Ives, "Indians Wounded in Fight at Wounded Knee . . . ," MS H84.38, Robinson Museum.)

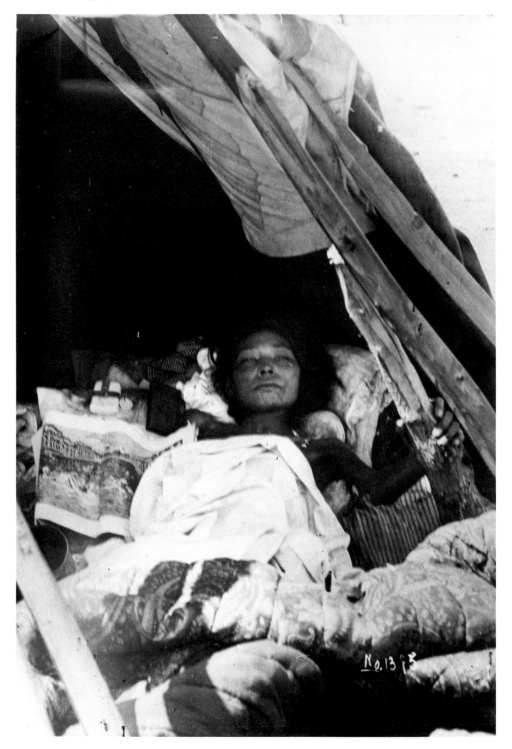

No. 13 75

90. Some of the wounded convalesced in the Miniconjou camp near the agency. Dr. Charles Eastman, a Santee who had treated some of the Indians later wrote, "[They] objected very strenuously to being treated by army surgeons, alleging as a reason that it was soldiers that had been the cause of their wounds, and they therefore never wanted to see a uniform again." (*Washington* (D.C.) *Evening Star*, Feb. 7, 1891.)

91. Some of the survivors escaped during the fighting and found refuge with the Ghost Dancers at the Stronghold. They were reunited with their kinsmen when the dancers surrendered in mid-January. *Addison E. Sheldon, editor of the* Chadron Advocate, *recalled the survivors he saw: "I still see them, the defeated, dejected Big Foot Sioux who were prisoners at Pine Ridge, December 31, 1890. It was near two o'clock in a gray, grimy morning as we drove . . . across White Clay Creek into the big yard in front of the Pine Ridge Agency. A band of men, women and children (mostly women and children) occupied the center of that yard. Some of them were prostrate on the ground. Some were sitting cross-legged, rocking to and fro in silent suffering. Some sat upon their ponies stiff and straight, but yet suffering."* (Addison E. Sheldon, "After Wounded Knee: A Recollection," 45.) ¶ The title assigned to this picture by the photographer for copyright purposes, "*What's left of Big Foot's band,*" may have been intended as an inducement to a potential buyer rather than an accurate identification. The group is the Crow Dog family of Rosebud, which was not present at Wounded Knee.

92. *Blue Whirlwind, a survivor of Wounded
Knee, said she had received fourteen wounds.
Two of her sons were also wounded. Her hus-
band, Spotted Thunder, was killed. Lois
Atwood, grand-niece of Clarence Moreledge,
identified Blue Whirlwind from another
Moreledge photograph in her possession.
(Atwood to Wendell Frantz, Curator
of Lincoln Museums, Nebraska State
Historical Society, Nov. 14, 1973.)*

93. *Brigadier General Leonard W. Colby holds his adopted daughter, Lost Bird. Colby commanded the Nebraska National Guard, which had been called out in response to the fears of settlers in northern Nebraska. By January 5 militia companies had arrived and positioned themselves between the reservations and the Nebraska railroad towns. When the Ghost Dancers surrendered to General Miles, the guardsmen were sent home. ¶ On January 14, General Colby went to the Pine Ridge Agency to confer with Miles. On this occasion Colby acquired Lost Bird, a nine-month-old girl said to have been orphaned at Wounded Knee. She became a celebrity when Colby took her to his Beatrice, Nebraska, home. On January 24, 1891, the Beatrice (Nebraska) Republican reported: "The general arrived home Saturday [January 18], with his newly acquired possession, and the following Sunday not less than 500 persons called at his house to see it. . . . The general has named the child Margaret Elizabeth, after the wives of the two brothers who helped him find it." ¶ A decade later Mrs. Colby petitioned the Bureau of Indian Affairs to have Lost Bird listed on the rolls of the Cheyenne River Agency and given full tribal rights, including an allotment of land. An investigation of the matter revealed that Lost Bird's mother, Rock Woman, had abandoned the child at Wounded Knee, believing she was dead. The child was found by the rescue party on January 1 and given to Yellow Bird, a Pine Ridge storekeeper. Yellow Bird located the baby's mother at the refugee camp, and the two were reunited. About this time Colby arrived, heard of the battlefield rescue, and expressed his wish to adopt the baby. At first Rock Woman objected, but after a few days she agreed. Colby gave her fifty dollars. (A. C. Towner to John R. Brennan, Aug. 7, 1901, Brennan Scrapbook, MS H72.2, folder 25, John R. Brennan Family Papers, Robinson Museum.)*

94. Father Francis M. J. Craft, S.J., a long-time missionary to the Indians, accompanied Forsyth's command to Wounded Knee on the evening of December 28. In a later statement, he said: "[I went] to see if I could be of any service, as malicious whites on and near all agencies, during the present excitement have, by misrepresenting the intentions of the Army, caused such a state of alarm and suspicion among the Indians as to make it possible for the least excitement or misunderstanding to participate [precipitate] serious trouble. I hoped to be of some service by going among the Indians and reassuring them." (Testimony of Reverend Francis M. J. Craft, *Army Investigations of Wounded Knee*.) ¶ Father Craft received a severe knife wound that pierced his right lung during the fighting at Wounded Knee. Despite his own wound he ministered to the wounded soldiers until he collapsed. Later, rancher James Cook described his recovery: "The wound he received would undoubtedly have killed some men. He was laid up for a short time, and if he stopped smoking cigarettes for two days because of that little cut, I have no record of it." (James H. Cook, *Fifty Years on the Old Frontier*, 204.) ¶ In this photograph he wears a silver medal of a fraternal order, signifying his rank as "Chief of the Senecas." (*Army and Navy Journal*, Jan. 3, 1891.)

The Mission Church   Bloody Pocket The Siege Mission Fight   Indians Viewing   No 1544

95. The day after Wounded Knee the Seventh Cavalry was again called to action. The Catholic mission shown here, which was four miles north of the Pine Ridge Agency, was reportedly on fire. Colonel Forsyth led his regiment to an intended rescue, but it turned out to be a rural day school burning instead. He met with sporadic resistance from Sioux snipers, who were well concealed in the broken terrain. Forsyth deployed his numerically superior force poorly, once again showing bad judgment in the field. His men were soon pinned down in the valley and threatened with encirclement. Only the timely arrival of the Ninth Cavalry in the midafternoon prevented this skirmish from becoming more serious. As it was, one officer and one private lost their lives. The number of Sioux warriors who participated could not be determined. ¶ The elements of this fight brought to observers' minds images of a beleaguered Seventh Cavalry at the Little Big Horn—which this time escaped a similar fate. Father Aemilius Perrig, a mission resident, remarked, "It seems there was an enormous waste of powder for nothing, which is no credit to either party's courage." (Father Aemilius Perrig, Diary, Dec. 30, 1890, Marquette University Library, Department of Special Collections and University Archives.)

96. The black Ninth Cavalry rode to the rescue of their white comrades pinned down near the mission. Major Guy V. Henry, an old veteran, led the detachment. The month of December had been a busy one for this regiment. It had been called on time and again to scout the Pine Ridge Reservation. At the time of the fight at Wounded Knee it, too, had been looking for Big Foot's band. When Henry learned of the fight and the threat to the agency, he turned back to provide support. "Henry's Ride," which covered over fifty miles in the bitter cold, brought him and his hardy troopers great acclaim. He later gave each of his men an engraved whistle, his trademark, as a memento of their accomplishment. ¶ No sooner had the exhausted column arrived at Pine Ridge on the morning of December 30 than they were called to arms again to ride to the mission. Little wonder that their exploits did nothing to dispel the romantic notion that the Sioux campaign was a continuation of the old Indian fighting army engaged in yet another Indian war.

97. The men of Troop K, Ninth Cavalry, posed here with their company guidon, participated in Henry's ride and the mission fight. They—and the other buffalo soldiers—distinguished themselves in both instances. ¶ Hostilities on the reservation did not cease with the mission fight. The last skirmish between the army and the Sioux occurred along the *White River* two days later, on January 1, when over one hundred men led by Two Strike attacked a wagon train of the Sixth Cavalry. Few casualties were suffered on either side.

98, 99. General Miles took command in the field on December 31. His arrival at Pine Ridge made an immediate impact. Wrote an anonymous observer, "The great air of secrecy which prevailed has disappeared, and he has communicated to his subordinates some general outline or plan of his campaign" (Letter from "Infantry," Pine Ridge Agency, Army and Navy Journal, Jan. 10, 1891.) Miles was especially displeased with the performance of Forsyth at Wounded Knee and the mission and, with the approval of Washington, launched an investigation. ¶ Left to right are Captain Ezra P. Ewers, Lieutenant John S. Mallory, Captain Francis E. Pierce, Lieutenant Colonel Dallas Bache, Captain Francis J. Ives, Major Jacob Ford Kent, Miles, Captain Frank D. Baldwin, Lieutenant Sydney A. Cloman, Captain Charles F. Humphrey, Captain Marion P. Maus, and Lieutenant Colonel Henry C. Corbin. An engraving of this photograph appeared in Frank Leslie's Illustrated Newspaper on February 7, 1891. ¶ Miles commanded such men as Buffalo Bill Cody, fresh from his failure to bring in Sitting Bull; Baldwin, who would head the Wounded Knee investigation; and longtime associate Maus. Colonel Eugene A. Carr, whose Sixth Cavalry had traveled from Fort Wingate, New Mexico, to participate in this campaign, is shown standing in the far right background.

Buffalo Bill

Capt. Baldwin

Gen N. A. Miles

Capt. Moss

Pine Ridge Agency S. D.

109

100. At the order of General Miles, Captain
William E. Dougherty, with two Hotchkiss
guns and two companies of the First Infantry,
set up a guard to the north of the agency. One
reporter sarcastically noted, "Instead of the
agency surrounding the soldiers, the soldiers
are to surround the agency." (St. Louis Post-
Dispatch, Jan. 4, 1891, dateline Jan. 3,
1891.) This photograph is remarkably similar to a January 24, 1891, Harper's
Weekly drawing by Frederic Remington,
entitled "In the Trenches at Pine Ridge—
From a Sketch Taken on the Spot."

101. *Artillery protected the agency from
attack. This cannon was of a larger caliber
than the pieces used at Wounded Knee. Miles,
like Brooke, was cautious about provoking
any further violence. He continued the strategy of tightening the cordon around the Sioux
while carrying out negotiations for surrender.*

102. Young Man Afraid of His Horses (on horseback) was a leading Oglala chief who supported the policies of the Bureau of Indian Affairs. In early November he obtained the necessary permission from Agent Royer to leave the reservation for a visit to the Crow tribe of Montana. At the request of Miles he rushed back by rail via Wyoming. The general hoped Young Man Afraid of His Horses could persuade the Ghost Dancers to surrender. On his January 7 return, he went to the Stronghold, where he was able to persuade many Oglalas to leave these camps and return to the agency. This set in motion a flood of defections that contributed to the final surrender of the Ghost Dancers on January 15.

103. Red Cloud returned to his home at Pine Ridge Agency on January 7. After the news of Wounded Knee, he had accompanied the stampeding throng, apparently against his will. Red Cloud told the military authorities later that he was prevented from leaving the camp at the Stronghold. With the help of his daughter, the enfeebled Sioux chief escaped and walked the many miles back to the agency. ¶ Red Cloud found that his home had been vandalized. He claimed that his property was "taken by Indians," sometime after December 29. Among the list of losses, no mention was made of the samurai sword hanging on the wall to the right of his blind wife. Its origin and disposition are unknown to historians. (Records of the Bureau of Indian Affairs, Record Group 75, "Records Relating to the Sioux Property Claims, 1891," claim no. 296, National Archives; and Peter Bleed, "Indians and Japanese Swords on the North Plains Frontier," 112–13.) An identical view, now in the collections of the University of Nebraska State Museum, was acquired by Major William J. Turner, Second Infantry, on December 7, 1890.

The "Bed Room" of American Horse.

104. The civilians at Wounded Knee were not the only Indian victims. The United States Congress appropriated one hundred thousand dollars in January 1891 to settle the property loss claims by Sioux Indians friendly to the government and legal residents on the Sioux reservations. Claims by Pine Ridge residents numbered 610, one of which was by American Horse, for losses suffered at the hands of the "disaffected" Brules and Oglalas. Most of the vandalism and thefts occurred just after the incident at Wounded Knee.

¶ American Horse was hit especially hard. He claimed losses amounting to $5,252.50, mostly livestock, of which only a third was allowed by the Indian Office. (Records of the Bureau of Indian Affairs, Record Group 75, "Records Relating to the Sioux Property Claims, 1891," claim no. 348, National Archives.) In the January 23, 1891, issue of the St. Louis Post-Dispatch, a reporter described his home: "American Horse had his house lined inside with cloth; a photograph of himself, neatly framed, hung upon the wall. There was a clock and a rocking chair, a cooking stove, and the bunks on which they slept were raised instead of being on the ground. . . . But because American Horse was friendly, the Brules went to his deserted home, tore down the cloth linings, threw his photograph on the floor, and shot holes through it, and utterly demolished every piece of furniture the house contained."

105, 106. *The cordon of cavalry around the camp at the Stronghold tightened. Infantry camps surrounded the agency. General Brooke (in the middle) and his troops, mostly Second Infantry, stood guard north of the agency, in the White River Valley. When the Indians began to trickle back, they camped within sight of the army. In the far background of the bird's-eye view, a tipi village can be seen. ¶ General Miles's daily dispatches to Washington noted the slow but steady progress of negotiations. Progress was literally measured in the number of miles that the Sioux camp moved each day toward the agency.*

107. After the Indians abandoned the Stronghold, they moved with extreme caution towards the Pine Ridge Agency. Camps were made after traveling only a few miles, while the leaders paused to reevaluate their situation. They feared the reception they would receive at the agency and were equally anxious about the intentions of soldiers who pressed close on their heels. Of great concern to the army were the political dramas being played out within the Sioux camps, away from the army's eyes. General Miles reported, "There is a report of heavy firing in or near the hostile camp that may be between the two elements of the Indian camp." (Miles to the Adjutant General, January 7, 1891, Army Investigations of Wounded Knee.)

108. From Captain Dougherty's vantage point came the first sighting of the returning Sioux on January 13: "The soldiers in Captain Dougherty's redoubts saw another grand spectacle. War-feeling evidently broke out afresh in the camp, for young warriors could be seen firing their rifles about the ears of the old men, who were doubtless counselling a surrender. Then they attacked their own horses and dogs, shooting them down in all directions. This demonstration was within twelve hundred yards of the great rifled cannon which peeps over the breastworks thrown up by Captain Dougherty." (Henry Davenport Northrop, Indian Horrors; or, Massacres by the Red Men, 599–600.)

109, 110. Defections from the Stronghold began during the second week of January. By the fifteenth the last of the Ghost Dancers had moved to the Pine Ridge Agency. On January 16, the Omaha World-Herald reported: "The Indians began to straggle in about noon. They are strung out along White Clay creek for a distance of two miles on foot, horseback and in wagons with a large number of ponies, some of them entering the friendlies' camp and some pitching their tepees on the west bank of White Clay creek. These are the Ogallalas. The Brules, however, are camping around Red Cloud's house on the bottoms. There are about 750 lodges with 3,500 Indians."

111. The newspaper account continued: "The entire valley for a distance of two miles on either side of the agency is occupied by tepees and immense herds of ponies cover all the hills as far as the eye can reach. The hostiles are all here and all declaring themselves friends of the government, all with good hearts and empty stomachs, and all desirous of carrying out the demands of General Miles."

112. Crow Dog was one of the more colorful figures before and during the time of the Ghost Dance. He was present when Crazy Horse was killed at Fort Robinson in 1877 and helped prevent a retaliatory attack on the soldiers. He was chief of police at the Rosebud Reservation in 1879–80 and became engaged in an unsuccessful opposition to Spotted Tail, the Brule chief. The political contest grew to hatred, and on August 5, 1881, he killed the chief. Blood money was paid to the heirs to settle the matter in traditional Brule fashion, but Crow Dog was convicted of murder in a Dakota Territory court. On appeal, the United States Supreme Court judged that the territory had no jurisdiction over the crime, which took place on the reservation, and Crow Dog was freed. ¶ Crow Dog was one of Short Bull's converts to the Ghost Dance. Crow Dog was adamantly opposed to the military occupation of the reservations, fled to the Stronghold, and declared that he would not return to his home until the army left. In mid-December he did surrender at Pine Ridge but returned to the Stronghold after the fighting at Wounded Knee. This photograph was taken on January 16 after yet another return to the agency.

113. Kicking Bear, a Ghost Dance leader, surrendered his rifle to Miles at the Pine Ridge Agency on January 15. With him came several thousand Sioux to camp near the agency. A reporter wrote: "Gen. Miles and his staff rode within twenty yards of the hostile camp to-day [January 17, not the sixteenth, as the photograph's caption says] to be photographed. His staff was afraid the General might be picked off, but he consented to go." (St. Louis Post-Dispatch, Jan. 18, 1891, dateline Jan. 17.) ¶ With the "war" at an end, demobilization began immediately. The members of the Nebraska National Guard were ordered back to their homes on January 13. Plans to disperse the regulars were initiated. The war machine would disappear almost as quickly as it had been formed.

114. George Trager seems to have chosen these persons carefully to represent the full spectrum of Lakota political and religious belief. Standing Bear (right) seems to epitomize the "progressive" Indian of the era, with his white-style clothing, watch chain, and Christian pin. Kicking Bear (left), the Ghost Dance leader, militantly advocated a return to the past Indian life style. Trager undoubtedly asked him to put his blanket on the ground so he could be seen wearing the traditional breechclout. Young Man Afraid of His Horses (middle) wears a mixture of Indian and white clothing, almost a symbol of his role as an intermediary.

Grand Council of Hostile and Friendly Sioux Indian Chiefs at Pine Ridge Agency S.D. Jan 17th 1891

Copy Righted Jan 30th 1891 by the North Western Photo Co Chadron Neb

Chief Young Man Afraid of his Horses talking

115, 116, 117. General Miles enlisted the aid of several Indian leaders to induce the surrendered Ghost Dancers to give up their weapons. A council was held on January 17, during which the Indians expressed their opinions on disarmament. Speakers included Kicking Bear, Two Strike, Young Man Afraid of His Horses, American Horse, Short Bull, High Pipe, and Standing Soldier. The only whites invited to speak were Lieutenant Taylor of the Indian scouts and ex-agent Valentine T. McGillycuddy. When the council concluded, only 104 guns were surrendered, but by the end of the month even the more belligerent dancers would concede to Miles's demands.

118. Lieutenant Charles William Taylor (seated, left) had witnessed the fight at Wounded Knee. His troop, composed of Oglalas and Cheyennes, had suffered one fatality. Seated to Taylor's left is Philip Wells, who appears, from the bandage on his nose, to be suffering still from the knife wound he received at Wounded Knee. The U.S. Army continued employing Indian scouts long after the campaign ended. Later in 1891 the army began its grand experiment of enlisting, equipping, and training Indians as regular soldiers, not just as scouts.

119. Robert White, an Oglala from Lieutenant Cloman's Troop C, posed for this Trager portrait. Although scouts were issued standard cavalry uniforms (note the United States Scouts hat insignia), White seems to have preferred a mixture of civilian and military attire. Trager used this backdrop for several outdoor portraits. It depicts an Indian war record and is done in Lakota-style artwork.

120. Lieutenant Cloman's troop of Indian scouts drill in a snowstorm. Cloman's scouts were Oglalas who had been recruited at Pine Ridge Reservation in late November 1890. They arrested Plenty Horses, a Brule, a month after he shot and killed Lieutenant Edward W. Casey, who had ventured too close to the Ghost Dance camp.

121. On January 7 Plenty Horses (center) shot Lieutenant Casey while the latter was in one of the Ghost Dance camps, trying to initiate peace talks. After his arrest, he was incarcerated at Fort Meade and brought to trial in Sioux Falls, South Dakota. Plenty Horses explained his actions: "I am an Indian. Five years I attended Carlisle and was educated in the ways of the white man. When I returned to my people, I was an outcast among them. I was no longer an Indian. I was not a white man. I was lonely. I shot the lieutenant so I might make a place for myself among my people. Now I am one of them. I shall be hung, and the Indians will bury me as a warrior. They will be proud of me. I am satisfied." (Julia B. McGillycuddy, McGillycuddy, Agent, 272.) Plenty Horses's lawyer successfully argued that the shooting was an act of war, for which he could not be punished in a civil court. He was sent home to Rosebud.

No. 3690½, Tasunka. Ota (alias Plenty Horse.) The slayer of Lieut. Casey, near Pine Ridge, S. Photo and copyright '91 by The Grabill P. & V. Co., Deadwood, S. D.

122. General Miles ordered the First Infantry's regimental band to play every day, which no doubt contributed to the military air of the agency. This concert was performed before Miles's headquarters, formerly the agent's residence. ¶ From here, on January 18, Miles announced to Washington and the world that the war was over. On the same day, officers Kent and Baldwin presented their findings to Miles and assigned some of the blame for the fight at Wounded Knee to Colonel Forsyth. Miles endorsed their reports but added harsh-er comments: "Incompetency and neglect, when found, should not pass unnoticed. . . . Warnings and orders were unheeded and disregarded by Colonel Forsyth." Miles's endorsement, dated January 31, 1891, was forwarded to the adjutant general, along with the reports of Major Kent and Captain Baldwin (Army Investigations of Wounded Knee). For Miles's superiors in Washington, however, the war both at Pine Ridge and in the ranks was indeed over. They ignored Miles's recommendations for punishment.

123. General Miles called for a "Grand Review" of his troops for January 21 and "sent word to the Indian chiefs that they must not look upon the movement of troops in the review as one directed against them, but rather as an evidence that the campaign is drawing to a close." (St. Louis Post-Dispatch, Jan. 20, 1891.) The review occurred two miles south of the agency. Over three thousand men took part. The First Infantry Band played "Garryowen" as the Seventh Cavalry passed by Miles. One reporter romantically described the review: "The column was almost pathetically grand, with its bullet-pierced gun-carriages, its tattered guidons, and its long lines of troopers and foot-soldiers facing a storm that was almost unbearable. It was the grandest demonstration by the army ever seen in the West; and when the soldiers had gone to their tents, the sullen and suspicious Brules were still standing like statues on the crests of the hills." (Charles G. Seymour, "The Final Review.")

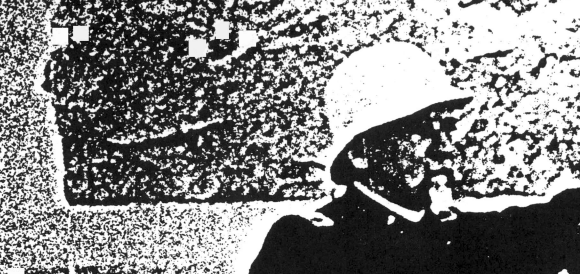

Epilogue

124. In this rather strange scene, the standing white man has donned a woman's beaded dress. His white colleague seated in front of him wears what appears to be a Ghost Dance shirt. With the formal cessation of hostilities, peace encouraged commerce and the proliferation of that most energetic and single-minded creature—the relic-hunter. On January 26 a newspaperman remarked, "If Gen. Miles had only given the relic hunters permission to visit the hostile camp there would have been no trouble." (St. Louis Post-Dispatch, Jan. 29, 1891, dateline Jan. 26.) Like locusts, white souvenir hunters cleaned out whole villages of their Indian-made artifacts. Prices for headdresses, pipes, beaded curios, and anything purportedly from Wounded Knee skyrocketed. Numerous Ghost Dance shirts carrying the attribution of being "the one worn by Big Foot" were sold. (Washington (D.C.) Evening Star, Feb. 9, 1891, dateline Feb. 1.)

125. Major Burke (front row, kneeling), of
Buffalo Bill's Wild West show, selected the
Sioux entertainers for the upcoming season.
Some believed that this opportunity for the
Sioux to see the world was one of the best
"civilizing" influences to exist. It was also
good business to bring before the public genu-
ine participants in the recent troubles.

126. *After the final surrender, twenty-seven Ghost Dancers were imprisoned at Fort Sheridan, Illinois, by order of Miles. The general believed that this group might lead a revival of the religion in the spring. They left Pine Ridge on January 26, expecting to spend six months at the army post near Chicago. ¶ Buffalo Bill Cody realized that such a group could become a feature attraction. Despite their imprisonment and the Bureau of Indian Affairs' ban on the employment of Indians by wild west shows, Cody used his considerable influence to secure their release. On March 30 twenty-three prisoners were placed in Cody's custody and they joined the show for a yearlong tour of Europe. Chicago photographer George E. Spencer identified these prisoners: (1) Crow Kane, (2) Medicine Horse, (3) Call Her Name, (4) Kicking Bear, (5) Short Bull, (6) Come and Grunt, (7) High Eagle, (8) Horn Eagle, (9) Sorrel Horse, (10) Scatter, (11) Standing Bear, (12) Lone Bull, (13) Standing Bear, (14) Close to House, (15) One Star, (16) Know His Voice, (17) Own the White Horse, (18) Take the Shield Away, (19) Brave.*

127. General Miles received permission to carry through on a request made to the Adjutant General on January 14, 1891. His proposal: "[I would like] to send a delegation to Washington to receive assurance of the higher authority of good intentions of the Government towards them. This will answer a double purpose, namely, satisfy them, bridge over the transition period between war and peace, dispel distrust and hostility, and restore confidence; it will also be a guarantee of peace while they are absent." (*Army Investigations of Wounded Knee*). ¶ The first group arrived at the nation's capital on January 29 and were joined by the rest of the delegation on February 1. They spent a week sightseeing, and purchased new suits at Saks', which were worn for the full delegation portrait. On the original photograph, these men are identified. First row, seated, left to right: High Hawk, Fire Lightning, Little Wound, Two Strike, Young Man Afraid of His Horses, Spotted Elk, Big Road. Second row, standing: F. D. Lewis, He Dog, Spotted Horse, American Horse, George Sword, Louis Shangreau, Bat Pourier. Third row: Dave Zephier, Hump, High Pipe, Fast Thunder, Rev. Charles Cook, P. T. Johnson.

128. The full delegation met with John W. Noble, secretary of the interior, and Thomas J. Morgan, the commissioner of Indian affairs. The Indians wanted Miles to be present, but he was not allowed to attend. The Interior Department feared he might voice pro-Indian sentiments embarrassing to the department. ¶ The Indians expressed a number of concerns, ranging from the army's actions at Wounded Knee to treaty obligations unfulfilled by the government. Secretary Noble assured the delegation that their concerns would receive attention, but the Indians were skeptical. After the conference Young Man Afraid of His Horses said: "We had some promises, but they were like all the other promises of the Great Father. We are not fooled and we go home with heavy hearts. . . . We shall tell our people that we have got more promises. Then they will laugh at us and call us old men." (Baltimore Sun, Feb. 19, 1891, in Herman J. Viola, Diplomats in Buckskins: A History of Indian Delegations in Washington City.) The original caption for the delegation's group portrait identifies: (1) Fire Lightning, (2) John Grass, (3) Two Strike, (4) Commissioner of Indian Affairs Thomas J. Morgan, (5) American Horse, (6) High Hawk, (7) High Pipe, (8) Young Man Afraid of His Horses, (9) Hollow Horn Bear, (10) Crazy Bear, (11) Medicine Bull, (12) White Ghost, (13) Quick Bear, (14) Little Wound, (15) Fast Thunder, (16) Spotted Horse, (17) Spotted Elk, (18) Grass, (19) Dave Zephier, (20) Louis Richard, (21) Clarence Three Stars, (22) Big Mane, (23) Big Road, (24) Hump, (25) Good Voice, (26) White Bird, (27) He Dog, (28) One to Play With, (29) Pete Lamont, (30) Wize, (31) No Heart, (32) Mad Bear, (33) Straight Head, (34) F. D. Lewis, (35) George Sword, (36) Turning Hawk, (37) Robert American Horse, (38) Rev. Luke Walker, (39) Bat Pourier, (40) Alex Recontreau, (41) Louis Shangreau.

129. Miles issued orders on January 26
that scattered his regiments to new stations.
The Eighth Infantry broke camp and moved
to Fort McKinney, Wyoming, its new regimental headquarters. The army saw no
need to abandon its strategy of stationing
large numbers of troops at forts located near
the Sioux reservations.

130. The First Infantry remained at the
agency for another month, until Miles
became satisfied that the threat of violence
had ended. On February 25 the regiment
boarded the train at Rushville to return to its
former station and a more hospitable climate
on the West Coast.

131. Four troops of the Ninth Cavalry
finally left Pine Ridge Agency on March
24. One trooper, W. A. Prather, the
regimental poet, set their plight to verse:

The rest have gone home,
And to meet the blizzard's wintry blast,
The Ninth, the willing Ninth,
Is camped here till the last.

We were the first to come,
Will be the last to leave,
Why are we compelled to stay,
Why this reward receive?

In warm barracks
Our recent comrades take their ease,
While we, poor devils,
And the Sioux are left to freeze.

And cuss our luck
And wait till some one pulls the string,
And starts Short Bull
With another ghost dance in the spring.
(Army and Navy Journal, Mar. 7, 1891.)

The Ninth's eagerness to leave probably
matched the wishes of the Sioux. A trooper
wrote: "The Indians complained that some
colored troops came to their camp, so they are
objecting to our color and prefer the whites.
This shows what civilization is doing." (Letter from "Decentralization," Pine
Ridge Agency, Army and Navy Journal,
Dec. 20, 1890.)

A Squaw Dance, P.R. Agency, S.D.
5/8-91

132. By May 8, 1891, it was not the Ghost Dance that was being performed, but other, "safer," dances. Although so-called Squaw Dances, exclusively by and for women, were common, the photographer's caption for this image may be incorrect. The center group of seated and bent women seems intent upon some activity on the ground, suggesting the women are playing a game of dice. Such games were popular, and the stakes were often high. The Presbyterian church on the east end of the main street of Pine Ridge looms in the background.

133, 134. *A large crowd of Indians and whites gathered at the Pine Ridge Agency for Fourth of July festivities. The commissioner of Indian affairs had grudgingly conceded that "as pastimes are a necessity of all people [the Sioux will] be permitted to engage in such innocent dances as the corn dances, squaw dances and the Omahas, the interdiction of which appears hardly judicious." This is probably an Omaha Dance.* (U.S. Commissioner of Indian Affairs, Sixtieth Annual Report, 1891, 183.)

135. General Cyrus Bussey, in his capacity
as assistant secretary of the interior, visited
the Pine Ridge Reservation six months after
the fight at Wounded Knee and held a council on July 3, 1891. He inspected the agency cattle herd, the annuity goods, and the
work that had been done by Captain
Charles G. Penney, the agent who had
replaced Royer. He carried back to Washington the knowledge and firsthand obser-
vations that the Ghost Dance was dead.

136. The summer of 1891 saw another group of government appointees come to the Sioux reservations. Congress had authorized a commission to solve the problems that had arisen when many of the Rosebud Indians refused to leave the Pine Ridge Reservation. Of the three members, Charles E. Pearce, Alpheus R. Appleman, and George H. Harries, the last had first-hand knowledge of the situation. Harries (third standing person from the left) had covered the past winter's troubles for the Washington (D.C.) Evening Star. Present at this gathering was the young John J. Pershing (standing, far left), first lieutenant in the Sixth Cavalry and later commanding general of the United States Army. He had recently been given command of a troop of Oglala soldiers. ¶ On June 27, 1891, the commissioners met at the Omaha Dance lodge at Wounded Knee. They heard Bull Eagle, a Sioux farmer, say: "My friends, this piece of land on the other side of the creek which has been flooded with blood is where I make my home. . . . Some men were killed right inside of my fence on the plowed ground. . . . I am still walking through the field and plowing up the ground, covering up the blood." (Letter . . . in relation to . . . South Dakota, 52nd Cong., 1st sess., 1891–92, Senate Ex. Doc. No. 58, 64.)

137. *As an epilogue, both sides dedicated monuments to their dead. The inscription of the Wounded Knee Monument at Fort Riley reads: "To the soldiers who were killed in battle with Sioux Indians at Wounded Knee and Drexel Mission, South Dakota, December 29 and 30, 1890. Erected as a tribute of affection by their comrades of the Medical Department and Seventh Cavalry, U.S. Army,* A.D. *1893."*

138. *In 1903 Joseph Horn Cloud, with help from friends and relatives, erected this monument at the side of the mass grave at Wounded Knee. The inscription reads in part: "Big Foot was a great Chief of the Sioux Indians. He often said I will stand in peace till my last day comes. He did many good and brave deeds for the white man and the Red Man. Many innocent women and children who knew no wrong died here."*

Notes

CHAPTER ONE

1. Elaine Goodale Eastman, "The Ghost Dance War and Wounded Knee Massacre of 1890–91," 28. For more recent anthropological examinations of the Ghost Dance, see Michael A. Sievers, "The Historiography of the 'Bloody Field' . . . That Kept the Secret of the Everlasting Word: Wounded Knee," 33–54; Raymond J. DeMallie, "The Lakota Ghost Dance: An Ethnohistorical Account," and Russell Thornton, *American Indian Holocaust and Survival.*

2. Father Aemilius Perrig, diary, Sept. 9 and 20, 1889, Marquette University Library, Department of Special Collections and University Archives. John M. Carroll, a noted authority on the Seventh Cavalry, brought this diary to our attention and graciously provided us with his transcription.

3. James Mooney, *The Ghost-Dance Religion and the Sioux Outbreak of 1890,* 764.

4. George Sword, "The Story of the Ghost Dance," 28; William T. Selwyn to E. W. Foster, Nov. 25, 1890, *Letter . . . relative to . . . Indians in certain States,* Senate Ex. Doc. No. 9, 51st Cong., 2nd sess., 1891, 35–36.

5. James McLaughlin, *My Friend the Indian,* 185–87.

6. Usher L. Burdick, *The Last Days of Sitting Bull,* 94–95; Sword, "Ghost Dance," 29.

7. Charles L. Hyde to Secretary of Interior John W. Noble, May 29, 1890, *Letter . . . relative to . . . Indians in certain States,* 51st Cong., 2nd sess., 1891, Senate Ex. Doc. No. 9, 3.

8. Warren K. Moorehead, "Ghost-Dances in the West," 327; Daniel Dorchester, "Report of the Superintendent of Indian Schools," Sept. 30, 1891, *Sixtieth Annual Report,* 1891, 529.

9. Louise P. Olson "Mary Clementine Collins, Dacotah Missionary," 77.

10. U.S. Commissioner of Indian Affairs, *Sixtieth Annual Report,* 1891, 530; Ellen Bradbury, Eileen Flory, and Moira Harris, *I Wear the Morning Star.*

11. See Rex Alan Smith, *Moon of Popping Trees,* 160; and Mooney, *Ghost-Dance Religion,* 916; *Army and Navy Journal,* Dec. 9, 1890, 243.

12. See George E. Bartlett, "Wounded Knee," MS8, Box 18, tablet 209, 8–9, Eli S. Ricker Collection, Nebraska State Historical Society. For the diffusion of the religion, see Mooney, *Ghost-Dance Religion.* For information about the Omaha Dance, see Clark Wissler, "Societies and Ceremonial Associations in the Oglala Division of the Teton-Dakota," 49. Wovoka demonstrated that he was bulletproof but it is not known whether the Lakota delegation witnessed the event. When a white official questioned him, Wovoka did not deny it but said it was a "joke" (A. I. Chapman to Gen. John Gibbon, Dec. 6, 1890, *Report of the Secretary of War . . . ,* 193).

13. Edmond G. Fechet, "The True Story of the Death of Sitting Bull," 500. For the anecdote about Porcupine, see Charles W. Allen, "In the West That Was: Memoirs, Sketches, and Legends," MS2635, 215, Nebraska State Historical Society.

14. A. P. Dixon to T. H. Ruger, Dec. 15, 1890, *Reports and Correspondence Relating to the Army Investigations of the Battle of Wounded Knee and to the Sioux Campaign of 1890–91,* National Archives Microfilm Publication M983 (hereafter cited as *Army Investigations of Wounded Knee*). Brigadier General Thomas H. Ruger to Assistant Adjutant General Merritt Barber, Nov. 26, 1890, *Report of the Secretary of War,* 189; T. H. Ruger, "Report of Operations Relative to the Sioux Indians in 1890 and 1891," Oct. 19, 1891, ibid., 179.

15. Reynolds to Commissioner of Indian Affairs, Nov. 2, 1890, *Letter . . . relative to . . . Indians in certain States,* 51st Cong., 2nd sess., 1891, Senate Ex. Doc. No. 9, 13; Palmer to Commissioner of Indian Affairs, Nov. 21, 1890, ibid., 28; Major General Nelson A. Miles to Adjutant General John C. Kelton, Nov. 19, 1890, *Army Investigations of Wounded Knee.*

16. Eastman, "Ghost Dance War," 33. Most contemporary writers and many later authors have cited Ghost shirts and armed dance guards as evidence of the militancy of the Ghost Dancers. In his article on the historiography of Wounded Knee, Michael A. Sievers concluded, "Advocates of the hostility thesis . . . are in the main either contemporaries of the event or history enthusiasts with little formal academic training in history" ("Historiography of the 'Bloody Field,'" 38). Sievers rightly left room for exceptions. Raymond J. DeMallie is one of a growing number of scholars who have con-

cluded that "when the record is evaluated objectively, it seems clear that the Lakota ghost dance did not have warlike intentions" ("Lakota Ghost Dance," *Pacific*, 394).

17. Robert V. Belt, Assistant Commissioner of Indian Affairs, to Daniel Royer, Nov. 14, 1890, *Letter . . . relative to . . . Indians in certain States*, 51st Cong., 2nd sess., 1891, Senate Ex. Doc. No.9, 21; A. T. Lea to J. A. Cooper, Nov. 22, 1890, ibid., 29; J. A. Cooper to R. V. Belt, Nov. 24, 1890, ibid., 30; Royer to Commissioner of Indian Affairs, Nov. 8, 1890, ibid., 44.

18. J. A. Cooper to R. V. Belt, Nov. 24, 1890, ibid., 30; Daniel Royer to T. J. Morgan, Nov. 9, 1890, ibid., 14; P. P. Palmer to T. J. Morgan, Nov. 28, 1890, ibid., 42; "Report of Major General Miles," Sept. 14, 1891, *Report of the Secretary of War*, 147.

19. Turning Hawk's Statement, Feb. 11, 1890, U.S. Commissioner of Indian Affairs, *Sixtieth Annual Report*, 1891, 179; *Omaha World-Herald*, Nov. 26, 1890.

20. *Omaha World-Herald*, Nov. 17 and Dec. 25, 1890.

21. Dunn, et al., Sept. 26, 1890, *Letter . . . relative to . . . Indians in certain States*, 51st Cong., 2nd sess., 1891, Senate Ex. Doc. No.9, 4; and Palmer to T. J. Morgan, Oct. 11, 1890, ibid., 14.

22. Ibid., Oct. 9, 1890, 9.

23. Ibid., Nov. 6, 1890, 13.

24. For information about the Eighth Cavalry's activities, see *Army and Navy Journal*, Nov. 22, 1890, 207; T. H. Ruger to Adjutant General, Oct. 19, 1890, *Report of the Secretary of War*, 180; and ibid., Nov. 26, 1890, 189.

25. Charles M. O'Connor to Sumner, Nov. 29, 1890, *Report of the Secretary of War*, 235; Sumner to N. A. Miles, Dec. 8, 1890, ibid., 228; "Report of Major General Miles," Sept. 14, 1891, ibid., 147; Assistant Adjutant General to Sumner, Dec. 16, 1891, ibid., 229.

26. E. V. Sumner to N. A. Miles, Dec. 23, 1890, ibid., 234; Donald F. Danker, "The Wounded Knee Interviews of Eli S. Ricker," 165, 181; N. A. Miles to Adjutant General, Dec. 30, 1890, *Army Investigations of Wounded Knee*, 635.

27. Sumner to N. A. Miles, Dec. 21, 1890, *Report of the Secretary of War*, 232; Sumner to N. A. Miles, Dec. 22 and 23, 1890, ibid., 233–34.

28. Dunn's statement of Jan. 17, 1891, ibid., 235–36;

Army and Navy Journal, Jan. 10, 1891, 337; Danker, "Wounded Knee Interviews," 185; Walter Mason Camp interview of Dewey Beard, n.d., Camp MSS, Box 6, f14, Lilly Library, Indiana University.

29. Danker, "Wounded Knee Interviews," 168, 185. Their decision to go to Pine Ridge was undoubtedly influenced by other factors. For example, Red Cloud and several other Oglala leaders invited Big Foot to come to their agency (ibid., 180). Sumner to Colonel H. C. Merriman, Dec. 27, 1890, *Report of the Secretary of War*, 211.

30. Danker, "Wounded Knee Interviews," 118, 170, 189.

31. Ibid., 190; Forsyth to Assistant Adjutant General, Dec. 31, 1890, *Army Investigations of Wounded Knee*, 760; Forsyth to Nelson Miles, Dec. 28, 1890, ibid., 743; Miles to Forsyth, Dec. 28, 1890, ibid.; Allen, In the West That Was, MS2635, 267, Nebraska State Historical Society.

32. Danker, "Wounded Knee Interviews," 172, 192, 222.

33. Ibid., 205; John C. Gresham, "The Story of Wounded Knee," 107.

34. Testimony of Robinson, Jan. 9, 1891, *Army Investigations of Wounded Knee*; George E. Bartlett, "An Awful Vengeance," MS8, box 18, tablet 209, Ricker Collection, Nebraska State Historical Society; James R. Walker, *Lakota Society*, ed. Raymond J. DeMallie, 165. Philip F. Wells witnessed this event and said it was "not as a signal to fight, but to illustrate the harmlessness of the soldiers' bullets" (Phillip F. Wells, "Ninety-six Years among the Indians of the Northwest," 303).

35. Danker, "Wounded Knee Interviews," 173, 192. Eyewitness accounts differ concerning this moment when the fighting started. The consensus opinion was that the first shot was accidental. For the statements of Frog and Elk Saw Him and the description by Wells, see Wells, "Ninety-six Years," 291, 293.

36. Allen "In the West That Was," MS2635, 272, Nebraska State Historical Society.

37. Testimony of Robinson, Jan. 9, 1891, *Army Investigations of Wounded Knee*; Allen, "In the West That Was," MS 2635, 280–81, Nebraska State Historical Society; George Sword, "Account Given by Indians of the Fight at

Wounded Knee Creek," Feb. 11, 1891, U.S. Commissioner of Indian Affairs, *Sixtieth Annual Report*, 1891, 180.

38. James McLaughlin, "Wounded Knee Compensation Papers," MSS H76.24, folder 14, page 20, Robinson Museum; Danker, "Wounded Knee Interviews," 178.

39. H. C. Merriman to Adjutant General, Dec. 25, 1890, *Report to the Secretary of War*, 209.

40. H. C. Merriman to Assistant Adjutant General, Jan. 30, 1891, ibid., 209; James McLaughlin, "Wounded Knee Interviews," MS Notebook 40, page 43, Assumption College Archives.

41. Frank D. Baldwin to Assistant Adjutant General, Feb. 5, 1891, *Army Investigations of Wounded Knee*, 1075–76. A blizzard and fear of an attack on the agency delayed the departure of the burial party; however, a hastily organized rescue party of Indians, including Dr. Charles Eastman, went to Wounded Knee, probably on January 1. Some accounts discuss these two parties as though they were one. For information about those who died at the Episcopal church, see Captain and Assistant Surgeon Francis Joseph Ives, MSS H84.38, Robinson Museum. For statements by Joseph Horn Cloud and others, see Danker, "Wounded Knee Interviews," 176–78 and McLaughlin, "Wounded Knee Compensation Papers," MS H76.24, folder 14, Robinson Museum.

42. Mooney, *Ghost-Dance Religion*, 868.

43. For Wells's account, see B. J. Peterson, *The Battle of Wounded Knee*, 19. For the statement of Elk Saw Him, see Wells, "Ninty-six Years," 293. *Washington* (D.C.) *Evening Star*, Jan. 28 and 30, 1891. Long Bull's statement is the only Indian account that specifically states there was a signal for the Indians to commence firing.

44. Danker, "Wounded Knee Interviews," 173; Walter Mason Camp, Interview with Good Thunder, July 12 and 13, 1912, Camp MSS, box 6, f14, Lilly Library, Indiana University.

45. Mooney, *Ghost-Dance Religion*, 880; Wells, "Ninty-six Years," 295. John R. Brennan Family Papers, MSS H72.2, folder 25, Robinson Museum. Yellow Bird, the storekeeper, assisted Colby in adopting a baby girl who survived Wounded Knee. The Cheyenne River Reservation census listed only three Yellow Birds: two young women

and a boy (C. E. McChesney, "Census of Cheyenne River Agency, S. D. Indians, June 30, 1890," Microcopy 595, roll 33, census nos. 30, 122, 466, National Archives Microfilm Publications).

CHAPTER TWO

1. Miles to Brooke, Nov. 17, 1890, reproduced in *Army Investigations of Wounded Knee*. This file, #5412-PRD-1890, brought together the records of the Kent-Baldwin Investigation into the conduct of Colonel Forsyth. It conveniently drew together nearly two thousand pages of documentation, not only from the War Department but also the Bureau of Indian Affairs, relating to the events leading to and including the Wounded Knee fight. These records, which are primarily correspondence, were used extensively in this research. Unless otherwise noted, the sources which follow came from this microfilm publication.

2. Robert M. Utley, *The Last Days of the Sioux Nation*, viii, 5, and 267, reflects this, as does Utley's later work, *Frontier Regulars: The United States Army and the Indian*, 1866–1891, xi, 397–413. The first book remains the standard work on Wounded Knee and was constantly consulted during the research for this work.

3. Jerry M. Cooper, "The Army's Search for a Mission, 1865–1890," in *Against All Enemies: Interpretations of American Military History from Colonial Times to the Present*, ed. Kenneth J. Hagan and William R. Roberts, 173–95; Paul Andrew Hutton, *Phil Sheridan and His Army*, 351. ¶ Few parallels have been drawn between the actions of the army to end the Ghost Dance and those to break up contemporaneous white "uprisings." Jerry M. Cooper's *The Army and Civil Disorder: Federal Military Intervention in Labor Disputes, 1877–1900* is a standard example of a study which excluded disturbances involving Indians and considered only those arising from the labor movement. Conversely, Robert Wooster's *The Military and United States Indian Policy, 1865–1903* considers labor disputes as a distraction to the army's main job. Both are excellent studies, but no middle ground seems to exist.

4. *Robert M. Utley, The Indian Frontier of the American West, 1846–1890, 201*, brings the Indian Wars to a close at

Skeleton Canyon, Arizona, on September 4, 1886.

5. For the standardized examples of the soldier's clothing and camp equipage, see Quartermaster General of the Army, *U.S. Army Uniforms and Equipment, 1889*, ed. Jerome A. Greene. Specifications for clothing and equipment, though similar to those of the 1870s, changed considerably by 1890.

6. Royer to the Commissioner of Indian Affairs, Oct. 30, 1890; ibid., Oct. 12, 1890.

7. Reynolds to the Commissioner of Indian Affairs, Nov. 2, 1890; Palmer to the Commissioner of Indian Affairs, Nov. 10, 1890.

8. Sitting Bull had to share this limelight somewhat with the Mormons of Utah, who were seen by some as the real behind-the-scenes instigators of the Messiah movement among the Indians. Gregory E. Smoak, "The Mormons and the Ghost Dance of 1890," 269–94.

9. Earnest to Brevet Lieutenant Colonel M. V. Sheridan, Department of the Platte, Omaha, Nov. 12, 1890; Miles to Major General John M. Schofield, Nov. 14, 1890.

10. President Harrison to Proctor, Nov. 13, 1890; Royer to the Commissioner of Indian Affairs, Nov. 13, 1890; George Chandler, Acting Commissioner of Indian Affairs, to Harrison, Nov. 13, 1890; Schofield to Miles, Nov. 14, 1890.

11. Royer to Brooke, Nov. 16, 1890; Brooke to Royer, Nov. 16, 1890, and reply from Royer, same date.

12. Dr. Charles A. Eastman recorded these words many years later in his autobiography, *From the Deep Woods to Civilization*, 94.

13. *Chicago Inter-Ocean*, Nov. 18, 1890, in an interview dated Nov. 17.

14. Miles to the Adjutant General, Washington, D.C., Nov. 19, 1890.

15. Miles to Brooke, Nov. 18 and 23, 1890, and Dec. 7, 1890.

16. *Omaha World-Herald*, Nov. 20, 1890, dateline Nov. 19. References in the newspapers made passing mention of a telephone line strung between the Pine Ridge Agency and Rushville. Why it played a seemingly minor role in the communications between Pine Ridge and the world is somewhat unclear, although the *Chicago Tribune* of No-

vember 23, 1890, noted that the telephone line was changed to one for telegraphic purposes because the former was "too slow and unreliable." Royer, who had the best access to the telephone, opted to travel to Rushville in person to use the telegraph for sensitive transmissions. Apparently Western Union's facilities far outshown those of an infant phone company. See also *Omaha World-Herald*, Dec. 1, 1890, and *Washington (D.C.) Evening Star*, Feb. 9, 1891. For information about the repair of the telegraph line, see *Chadron (Nebraska) Advocate*, Nov. 21, 1890, and *Omaha World-Herald*, Nov. 22, 1890. For information about Western Union's assistance, see *Omaha World-Herald*, Nov. 20, 1890. *Omaha Bee*, Nov. 27, 1890, dateline Nov. 26.

17. Assistant Adjutant General Chauncey M. McKeever to Merritt, Nov. 20, 1890; Schofield to Merritt, Nov. 21, 1890; Schofield to McCook, Nov. 21, 1890; Schofield to Miles, Nov. 22, 1890; McKeever to Miles, Nov. 22, 1890, relaying authorization from Proctor and Schofield.

18. *Omaha Bee*, Nov. 20, 1890; *Omaha World-Herald*, Nov. 23, 1890; *Nebraska State Journal* (Lincoln), Nov. 25, 1890.

19. Schofield to Miles, Nov. 22, 1890; Merritt to the Adjutant General, Nov. 24, 1890; Miles to the Adjutant General, Nov. 22, 1890; Lieutenant Colonel Alfred T. Smith, Rosebud Agency, to Miles, Nov. 26, 1890.

20. Schofield to McCook, Nov. 30, 1890; Captain Lafayette E. Campbell, Quartermaster for the Sixth U.S. Cavalry, Denver, to the Quartermaster General, Washington, D.C., Dec. 5, 1890. The quartermaster general's office calculated the cost of the campaign to be one million, three hundred thousand dollars, with nine hundred thirty-five thousand dollars going toward transportation (*Army and Navy Journal*, Feb. 7, 1891).

21. Schofield to the Commanding Generals of the Departments of the Pacific, the Missouri, and Texas, Dec. 1, 1890; Schofield to Miles, Dec. 2 and 3, 1890; Brigadier General Charles Sutherland, "Report of the Surgeon General, September 22, 1891," *Report of the Secretary of War*, 599–603.

22. Miles to the Adjutant General, with a report from Ruger, Nov. 25, 1890; Palmer to the Commissioner of In-

dian Affairs, Dec. 1, 1890; Miles to the Adjutant General, Nov. 28, 1890. This point was reiterated in Miles's article, "The Future of the Indian Question," 1–10.

23. Proctor to Miles, with instructions from Harrison, Dec. 1, 1890.

24. *Army and Navy Journal*, Dec. 27, 1890.

25. *Omaha World-Herald*, Nov. 30, 1890, dateline Nov. 29.

26. Adjutant General to Miles, with authorization from the Secretary of War to hire Indians, Dec. 1, 1890; Allen, "In the West That Was," MS2635, Nebraska State Historical Society; *St. Louis Post-Dispatch*, Jan. 14, 1891; Miles to the Adjutant General, with telegrams from Brooke, Dec. 7, 1890.

27. Miles to the Commanding Officer of Fort Yates, Nov. 30, 1890. An interesting eyewitness account of this episode is by Major Matthew Forney Steele, "Buffalo Bill's Bluff," 475–85. Miles lodged a complaint about McLaughlin's interference: "I will endeavor to secure the person of that Indian, but it will be more difficult now than before." (Miles to Schofield, Dec. 6, 1890.)

28. Assistant Adjutant General Henry C. Corbin to the Adjutant General, Dec. 16, 1890, with a copy of the arrest order for Sitting Bull of Dec. 10. ¶ The primary eyewitness account of the arrest and killing of Sitting Bull is by Captain Edmond G. Fechet, Eighth Cavalry, to the Post Adjutant, Fort Yates, Dec. 17, 1890. Fechet commanded the detachment of troops that morning. He later prepared two lengthier versions, "Death of Sitting Bull," 493–501, and "The Capture of Sitting Bull," 185–93.

29. Corbin to the Adjutant General, with a telegram from Brooke, Dec. 15, 1890; *Army and Navy Journal*, Dec. 20, 1890; Palmer to the Commissioner of Indian Affairs, Dec. 17, 1890; Miles to the Adjutant General, Dec. 22, 1890; *Army and Navy Journal*, Dec. 27, 1890.

30. Miles to the Adjutant General, Dec. 13, 1890.

31. "Report of Major General Miles," Sept. 14, 1891, *Report of the Secretary of War*, 147.

32. Assistant Adjutant General, Chicago, to Schofield, Nov. 29, 1890; Miles to Schofield, Dec. 12, 1890; *Omaha Bee*, Dec. 18, 1890, dateline Dec. 17 from Rapid City.

33. *Army and Navy Journal*, Mar. 7, 1891.

34. *Omaha Bee*, Dec. 29, 1890, dateline Dec. 28; Miles to the Adjutant General, with Sumner's report of Big Foot's capture, Dec. 22, 1890; Ruger to the Adjutant General, Dec. 22, 1890.

35. Ruger to the Adjutant General, Dec. 27, 1890, with telegrams from Sumner, *Army Investigations of Wounded Knee*; Report of Lieutenant Colonel E. V. Sumner, Feb. 3, 1891, "Report of Operations Relative to the Sioux Indians in 1890 and 1891," *Report of the Secretary of War*, 223–38; Miles to the Adjutant General, Dec. 24, 1890; Testimony of Brooke before the Kent-Baldwin Investigation, Jan. 17, 1891; "Report of Major General Miles," 147–48, 150.

36. Miles to the Adjutant General, with Brooke's telegram of the same date, Dec. 28, 1890; Schofield to Miles, Dec. 29, 1890.

37. Miles to the Adjutant General, with three Brooke telegrams, Dec. 29, 1890.

38. *Army and Navy Journal*, Jan. 17, 1891, from the Junction City (Kansas) *Republican*.

39. Miles to the Adjutant General, with Brooke's report, Dec. 30, 1890; Schofield to Miles, Chadron, Dec. 30, 1890.

40. *Omaha Bee*, Dec. 31, 1890; *Army and Navy Journal*, Jan. 10, 1891.

41. W. L. Holloway, *Wild Life on the Plains and Horrors of Indian Warfare*, 590.

CHAPTER THREE

1. Paula Richardson Fleming and Judith Lusky, *The North American Indians in Early Photographs*, 192–96.

2. The Federal Census of 1880 shows Trager, age nineteen, living with his brother, Charles, and his family in Mazomanie, Wisconsin. See also Elmo Scott Watson, "Some Notes on the Photographers of the Ghost Dance Troubles in South Dakota, 1890–91," Elmo Scott Watson Collection, Newberry Library. Also, the State Historical Society of Wisconsin is compiling a directory of photographers in that state. Information from that directory was provided in a personal communication from Geraldine Strey, Research Librarian, on September 8, 1989.

3. *Chadron (Nebraska) Democrat*, Apr. 24, 1890.

4. David Seidel, *Fremont, Elkhorn & Missouri Valley Railroad Company*, 22–33. See also "The Fremont, Elkhorn & Missouri Valley Railway," *Omaha Bee*, Dec. 14, 1890.

5. *Chadron (Nebraska) Democrat*, Apr. 24, 1890; "Ernest G. Trager Succumbs Here to Extended Illness," *Casper (Wyoming) Herald*, Oct. 9, 1928.

6. "Pilgrims to Pine Ridge," *Chadron (Nebraska) Advocate*, Mar. 14, 1890; *Chadron (Nebraska) Democrat*, Mar. 13, 1890.

7. The *Chadron (Nebraska) Democrat* of June 19, 1890, gives a sense of the volume of business that the firm was doing: "B. F. Kuhn, the Crawford member of Trager & Kuhn, photographers of this city, was here the latter part of the week finishing up three or four hundred pictures from their Crawford branch."

8. *Chadron (Nebraska) Democrat*, Sept. 25, 1890.

9. The *State Business Gazetteer* shows J. S. Meddaugh in only the 1890–91 edition, though other photographers appear in that town before and after those years. Other examples of his work suggest that he may have been in Rushville as early as 1888. (*Nebraska State Gazetteer, Business Directory and Farm List for 1890–1891*, vol. 3, [Omaha, Nebr.: J.M. Wolfe and Co., 1890].)

10. *Chadron (Nebraska) Democrat*, Oct. 23, 1890.

12. *Omaha Bee*, Nov. 19, 1890. In the *Omaha Bee* of November 19, 1890, Cressey reports, "Representatives of the Chicago Times and Herald joined our train at Fremont and more than a dozen others from leading papers in the east are trailing us one train in the rear of ours." See also the *Omaha World-Herald*, Nov. 19, 1890. Moreledge's presence on the train is speculation, based on his appearance on the reservation simultaneously with the reporters. In a later story, printed January 13, 1891, in the *World-Herald*, Carl Smith states that Moreledge is in the employ of the paper.

12. *Omaha Bee*, Nov. 20, 1890. Even papers that had dispatched correspondents to the trouble area carried Cressey's reports. One can only wonder why, with the reservation packed with seventeen or more reporters— even one from the Associated Press—Cressey's stories were the ones that were published nationally.

13. *Omaha World-Herald*, Nov. 21, 1890. Smith detailed his first encounter with Royer in a later article, published in the *Omaha World-Herald* on December 1, 1890. "On the day of my arrival I found the agent (Royer) at his post in the agency at Rushville in an upstairs room of a hotel where he was doing a lot of writing. Meanwhile, the stage, driven by a lone young man, continued to run between the agency and the town, although the agent found it convenient to come in. He said that the Indians were so bad that he did not dare use his telephone for fear that they would learn of the coming of the troops and so he came over of nights to transmit what information he had."

14. *Ibid.*, Nov. 21, 1890. Also, an article in the February 9, 1891, *Washington (D.C.) Evening Star* details the difficulty that reporters had getting their stories to their home offices.

15. *Chadron (Nebraska) Advocate*, Nov. 21 and 28, 1890.

16. All of Cressey's articles in the *Bee* are overblown, but the one that appeared on the front page of the November 22, 1890, issue (dateline Nov. 21, 1890) is particularly appropriate to illustrate his penchant for yellow journalism. In it he reports that nothing had happened that night, but the article begins with the following sentence: "The dawn of another day has come and mercifully without bloodshed in our midst." ¶ A good example of one of Smith's articles may be found in the *Omaha World-Herald*, Nov. 25, 1890. Also, in an article in the November 26 issue (dateline Nov. 25) Smith says: "I desire to say that Agent Royer has twice threatened to expel me from the agency if criticisms of his conduct of the agency are published. He says that there is not a thing in my reports which is not fair and impartial, but if the *World-Herald* continues to speak of him as inexperienced or frightened, he will deny the [paper] representation here."

17. *Chadron (Nebraska) Democrat*, Nov. 27, 1890.

18. "A Visit to the Front," *Chadron (Nebraska) Advocate*, Nov. 28, 1890.

19. *Ibid.*

20. *Ibid.*

21. *Omaha World-Herald*, Nov. 28, 1890, dateline November 27, 1890.

22. *Omaha World-Herald*, Dec. 1, 1890. There is no offi-

cial announcement of Smith's expulsion. Smith simply disappeared. The reports in subsequent issues of the *World-Herald* appear without a by-line until Thomas Tibbles begins his reports in the December 7, 1890, issue. Smith ended his last article before exile (dated December 1, 1890) with the following: "To hold his job Mr. Royer may succeed in aggravating these Indians into some sort of warlike demonstration, but it will be fighting against their will. They are not fools, and do not desire to make a winter fight with no forage in sight."

23. *Omaha World-Herald*, Nov. 28, 1890, dateline November 27, 1890; *Chadron (Nebraska) Democrat*, Dec. 4, 1890, dateline Nov. 30, 1890.

24. R. J. Boylan, Jr., of the *St. Louis Post-Dispatch*, observed (Dec. 11, 1890), "At Rushville the only inhabitants who were sufficiently composed to attend to business were the hotel runners, who plied their vocation as if they considered this Indian trouble to be a special dispensation of Providence in the interest of the hotel business." ¶ The *Chadron Democrat* of December 4, 1890, describes Trager's activities. Moreledge's photograph first appeared in the November 30, 1890, issue of the *Chicago Inter-Ocean*, and within a fortnight had appeared in the *Omaha World-Herald*, the *New York Herald*, and the *St. Louis Post-Dispatch*.

25. *Chadron (Nebraska) Democrat*, Dec. 18, 1890.

26. "War on the Wounded Knee," *Chadron (Nebraska) Advocate*, Jan. 2, 1891.

27. *Chadron (Nebraska) Democrat*, Jan. 8, 1891.

28. "War on the Wounded Knee," *Chadron (Nebraska) Advocate*, Jan. 2, 1891.

29. *Ibid*. One can only imagine the delight that A. E. Sheldon took in the suffering of his dry comrades, as he was a staunch and vocal prohibitionist.

30. *Ibid*.

31. *Ibid*.

32. *Ibid*.

33. *Ibid*.

34. *Chadron (Nebraska) Democrat*, Mar. 22, 1888, Apr. 5, 1888, and Dec. 19, 1889.

35. *Chadron (Nebraska) Democrat*, May, 9, 1889. By this time Thomas Tibbles's wife, Suzette LaFlesche Tibbles, was writing for the *Omaha World-Herald* under her Indian name, Bright Eyes. In her column for that paper of December 18, 1890 (dateline December 17, 1890) she notes, "Some one has started up a barber shop, and the door being open and some men being shaved, two Indian women passing by looked in and seemed very much amused, never having seen anyone shaved before, and soon there was a crowd around the door chattering and laughing over the performance." See also "War on the Wounded Knee," *Chadron (Nebraska) Advocate*, Jan. 2, 1891.

36. *Chadron (Nebraska) Democrat*, Jan. 8, 1891.

37. *Ibid*.

38. *Ibid*. The story of S. D. Butcher's trip to Pine Ridge is taken from an article entitled "Photographing Indians," which was published in the *West Union (Nebraska) Gazette*. Butcher extracted this article and published it as the introduction to the backlist of his Wounded Knee–related photographs. The actual newspaper containing this article is not extant, and therefore no date for it is available. In notes annotating his collection at the Nebraska State Historical Society he reported that he and Orvis spent twenty-two days on the road to make these pictures.

39. *West Union (Nebraska) Gazette*, "Photographing Indians."

40. *Chadron (Nebraska) Advocate*, Jan. 9, 1891.

41. *Chadron (Nebraska) Democrat*, Jan. 15, 1891.

42. *Ibid*.

43. Watson, "Notes on Photographers," 3, Watson Collection, Newberry Library.

44. *Omaha World-Herald*, Jan. 14, 1891, dateline Jan. 13, 1891.

45. A dispatch from George H. Harries of the *Washington (D.C.) Star* dated February 9, 1891, reads, "The faraway artists [meaning Butcher, Grabill, and Cross] had no opportunity at all [to get battlefield pictures], but Messrs. Trager & Kuhn of Chadron, Neb. managed to get there with profitable promptitude. It was hard work to supply the local demand for the pictures they took and for a while quite impossible to fill the orders that tumbled in from all parts of the country. When the battle grounds and the earthworks and the buildings had been photographed then commenced the lucre-catching job of mak-

ing pictures of the army by companies [such as plate 139, above]. Of course every soldier wanted all the scenes of war and at least one copy of the photograph in which he was a figure. There was money in that business." Piper to his wife, Jan. 11, 1891, Alexander R. Piper, "Extracts from Letters Written by Lieutenant Alexander R. Piper . . . during the Sioux Campaign, 1890–1891," *The Unpublished Papers of the Order of Indian Wars Book Number 10*, 16.

46. *Omaha World-Herald*, Nov. 29, 1890; Watson, "Notes on Photographers," Watson Collection, Newberry Library.

47. William Powers, "The Sioux Omaha Dance," 30. In this article a photograph of five dancers who were identified as members of Big Foot's band was published. The picture was located by Richard Conn of the Denver

Art Museum. Mr. Conn had obtained the photograph from the Eastern Washington State Historical Society. Prints found in that institution's collections bore inscriptions positively identifying the group as members of Big Foot's band.

48. Charles Collins, comp., *Collins' Omaha City Directory*, 202; Solomon Deaper, "History of Knox County," 2–6. This attribution is based on a number of images from the Bailey, Dix, and Mead series that appear on Cross mounts. One particularly good example may be found at the South Dakota State Historical Society at Pierre. In an October 30, 1942, letter to Martha Turner (the woman in charge of the photographic collections for the Nebraska State Historical Society), Leona Dix Wilber wrote, "I have been trying to find out more about the history of these

views but so far can only tell you my father Dr. Geo. P. Dix was at Ft. Randall doing dentistry for the U.S. troops there when he and the other two men had these pictures taken [and] they sold some."

49. Henry W. Hamilton and Jean Tyree Hamilton, *The Sioux of the Rosebud: A History in Pictures*, 4.

50. The Hot Springs (South Dakota) *Daily Star* of January 30, 1891, made note of Cross's activities: "W. R. Cross has been over to Pine Ridge for a few days past, 'taking' the Injuns. He returned this morning."

51. Chadron (Nebraska) *Advocate*, Feb. 20, 1891.

52. Chadron (Nebraska) *Advocate*, Jan. 23, 1891; Chadron (Nebraska) *Democrat*, Jan. 29, 1891. There are two possible interpretations of Joe Ford's sale of Big Foot's Ghost Dance shirt. The Chadron (Nebraska) *Advocate* of January 30, 1891, reads, "Also Big Chief Joe Ford, who goes along in the interest of the Northwestern Photograph Company, and will sell Wounded Knee pictures and the ghost shirt worn by Big Foot to several thousand credulous eastern natives." It could mean either that Ford had Big Foot's shirt, or that he carried a supply of fake shirts, of which there was a proliferation, for sale to a gullible eastern market.

53. Chadron (Nebraska) *Advocate*, Feb. 13 and 20, 1891; Chadron (Nebraska) *Democrat*, Feb. 12 and 19, 1891; Chadron (Nebraska) *Advocate*, June 5, 1891.

54. Chadron (Nebraska) *Democrat*, Mar. 5, 1891.

55. Ibid., Mar. 19 and Apr. 2, 1891.

56. Chadron (Nebraska) *Advocate*, May 1, 1891; Chadron (Nebraska) *Democrat*, May 7, 1891; George D. Watson, Jr., *Prairie Justice 1885–1985: A One Hundred Year Study of the Legal System of Chadron and Dawes County*, 175.

57. Chadron (Nebraska) *Citizen*, July 21, 1892. A note in the *Dawes County (Nebraska) Journal*, May 27, 1892, suggests that Trager had attempted to open a studio in Gordon, Nebraska, during that time as well.

58. Chadron (Nebraska) *Citizen*, Aug. 4, 1892; Chadron (Nebraska) *Democrat*, Oct. 11, 1892; Fremont (Nebraska) *Tri-Weekly*, May 11, 1893.

59. Moreledge to A. M. Dockery, Feb. 16, 1904. This letter is attached to Moreledge's commutation papers, Office of the Secretary of State, State of Missouri, Jefferson City, Missouri.

60. Governor A. M. Dockery to the Secretary of the State of Missouri, Aug. 2, 1904, letter attached to the commutation papers for Clarence Moreledge, Office of the Secretary of State, State of Missouri, Jefferson City, Missouri. Lois Atwood to the Smithsonian Institution, Oct. 9, 1973, correspondence file of the National Anthropological Archives, Smithsonian Institution, Washington, D.C. Lois Atwood was Moreledge's grandniece, who in the early 1970s was doing biographical research on her great-uncle.

61. Watson, "Notes on Photographers," Watson Collection, Newberry Library. See also donor records, Photographic Collections, Nebraska State Historical Society.

62. Watson, "Notes on Photographers," 3, Watson Collection, Newberry Library; "Ernest G. Trager Succumbs Here to Extended Illness," *Casper (Wyoming) Herald*, Oct. 9, 1928.

References

MANUSCRIPTS

Assumption College Archives, Richardton, North Dakota
McLaughlin, James. "Wounded Knee Interviews." MS Notebook 40.

Colorado Historical Society, Denver, Colorado
DuBois, George B. MS no.215, box 1.

Indiana University, Lilly Library, Bloomington, Indiana
Camp, Walter Mason.

Marquette University Library, Department of Special Collections and University Archives, Milwaukee, WI
Perrig, Father Aemilius. Diary.

National Archives, Washington, D.C.
Records of the Bureau of Indian Affairs. Record Group 75. "Records Relating to Sioux Property Claims, 1891."

Nebraska State Historical Society, Lincoln, Nebraska
Allen, Charles W. "In the West That Was: Memoirs, Sketches, and Legends." MS2635.
Ricker, Eli S. MS8.

Newberry Library, Chicago, Illinois
Watson, Elmo Scott. "Some Notes on the Photographers of the Ghost Dance Troubles in South Dakota, 1890–91." Elmo Scott Watson Collection.

Robinson Museum, Pierre, South Dakota
Brennan, John R. Family Papers. MS H72.2, folder 25.
Ives, Francis Joseph. "Indians Wounded in Fight at Wounded Knee, South Dakota, December 29, 1890, Treated by Frank J. Ives, Capt. & Asst. Surgeon, USA." MSS H84.38.
McLaughlin, James. "Wounded Knee Compensation Papers." MSS H76.24, folder 14.

GOVERNMENT REPORTS

McChesney, C. E. "Census of Cheyenne River Agency, S.D. Indians, June 30, 1890." Microcopy 595, roll 33. National Archives Microfilm Publications.

Report of the Secretary of War; Being Part of the Message and Documents Communicated to the Two Houses of Congress at the Beginning of the First Session of the Fifty-Second Congress. Vol.1 of 5. Washington, D.C.: GPO, 1892.

Reports and Correspondence Relating to the Army Investigations of the Battle of Wounded Knee and to the Sioux Campaign of 1890–91. National Archives Microfilm Publication M983.

U.S. Commissioner of Indian Affairs. Fifty-Ninth Annual Report, 1890. Washington, D.C.: GPO, 1890.
———. Sixtieth Annual Report, 1891. Washington, D.C.: GPO, 1891.

U.S. Congress. Senate. Letter . . . in relation to . . . South Dakota. 52nd Cong., 1st sess., 1891–92. Senate Ex. Doc. No.58.

U.S. Congress. Senate. Letter . . . relative to . . . Indians in certain States. Senate Ex. Doc. No.9. 51st Cong., 2nd sess., 1891.

PERIODICALS

Army and Navy Journal
Beatrice (Nebraska) Republican
Casper (Wyoming) Herald
Chadron (Nebraska) Advocate
Chadron (Nebraska) Citizen
Chadron (Nebraska) Democrat
Chicago Inter-Ocean
Chicago Tribune
Dawes County (Nebraska) Journal
Frank Leslie's Illustrated Newspaper
Fremont (Nebraska) Tri-Weekly
Harper's Weekly
Hot Springs (South Dakota) Daily Star
Nebraska State Journal (Lincoln)
New York Herald
New York World
Omaha Bee
Omaha World-Herald
St. Louis Post-Dispatch
Washington (D.C.) Evening Star

BOOKS AND ARTICLES

Andrews, Ralph W. Indians as the Westerners Saw Them. Seattle: Superior Publishing Co., 1963.

Beyer, W. F., and O. F. Keydel, eds. Deeds of Valor. Vol.2. Detroit: 1907.

Bleed, Peter. "Indians and Japanese Swords on the North Plains Frontier." Nebraska History 68, no.3 (1987): 112–15.

Bradbury, Ellen, Eileen Flory, and Moira Harris. I Wear the Morning Star. Minneapolis: Minneapolis Institute of Arts, 1976.

Burdick, Usher L. *The Last Days of Sitting Bull.* Baltimore: Wirth Brothers, 1941.

Collins, Charles, comp. *Collins' Omaha City Directory.* Omaha: The Omaha-Herald Book and Job Office, 1868.

Cook, James H. *Fifty Years on the Old Frontier.* Norman: University of Oklahoma Press, 1957.

Cooper, Jerry M. *The Army and Civil Disorder: Federal Military Intervention in Labor Disputes, 1877–1900.* Westport, Conn.: Greenwood Press, 1980.

———. "The Army's Search for a Mission, 1865–1890." In *Against All Enemies: Interpretations of American Military History from Colonial Times to the Present.* Edited by Kenneth J. Hagan and William R. Roberts. Westport, Conn.: Greenwood Press, 1986.

Danker, Donald F. "The Wounded Knee Interviews of Eli S. Ricker." *Nebraska History* 62 (1981): 151–243.

Draper, Solomon. "History of Knox County." *Niobrara Pioneer,* July 20, 1876, 2–6.

DeMallie, Raymond J. "The Lakota Ghost Dance: An Ethnohistorical Account." *Pacific Historical Review* 51, no.4 (1982): 385–405.

Eastman, Charles A. *From the Deep Woods to Civilization.* 1936. Reprint. Lincoln: University of Nebraska Press, 1977.

Eastman, Elaine Goodale. "The Ghost Dance War and Wounded Knee Massacre of 1890–91." *Nebraska History* 26, no.1 (1945): 26–42.

———. *Sister to the Sioux: The Memoirs of Elaine Goodale Eastman, 1885–91.* Edited by Kay Graber. Lincoln: University of Nebraska Press, 1978.

Fechet, Edmond G. "The Capture of Sitting Bull." *South Dakota Historical Collections* 4 (1908): 185–93.

———. "The True Story of the Death of Sitting Bull." *Cosmopolitan* 20 (Mar. 1896): 493–501. (Reprinted in *Proceedings and Collections of the Nebraska State Historical Society,* second series, 2 [1898]: 179–90.)

Fiske, Frank Bennett. *Life and Death of Sitting Bull.* Fort Yates, N.Dak.: Pioneer Arrow Print, 1933.

Fleming, Paula Richardson, and Judith Lusky. *The North American Indians in Early Photographs.* New York: Harper and Row, 1986.

Gresham, John C. "The Story of Wounded Knee." *Harper's Weekly,* Feb. 7, 1891.

Hamilton, Henry W., and Jean Tyree Hamilton. *The Sioux of the Rosebud: A History in Pictures.* Norman: University of Oklahoma Press, 1971.

Hettinger, August. "Personal Recollections of the 'Messiah Craze Campaign.'" *Winners of the West,* Jan. 30, 1935.

Holloway, W. L. *Wild Life on the Plains and Horrors of Indian Warfare.* St. Louis: Excelsior Publishing Co., 1891.

Hutton, Paul Andrew. *Phil Sheridan and His Army.* Lincoln: University of Nebraska Press, 1985.

Johnson, W. Fletcher. *Life of Sitting Bull and the History of the Indian War of 1890–91.* Philadelphia: Edgewood Publishing Co., 1891.

Lindberg, Christer. "Foreigners in Action at Wounded Knee." *Nebraska History* 71, no.4 (1990): 170–81.

McGillycuddy, Julia B. *McGillycuddy, Agent.* 1941. Reprinted as *Blood on the Moon.* Lincoln: University of Nebraska Press, 1990.

McLaughlin, James. *My Friend the Indian.* 1916. Reprint. Lincoln: University of Nebraska Press, 1989.

Miles, Nelson A. "The Future of the Indian Question." *North American Review* no.410 (Jan. 1891): 1–10.

Mooney, James. *The Ghost-Dance Religion and the Sioux Outbreak of 1890.* Fourteenth Annual Report of the Bureau of Ethnology, Smithsonian Institution. Washington, D.C.: Government Printing Office, 1896.

Moorehead, Warren K. "Ghost-Dances in the West." *Illustrated American,* Jan. 17, 1891.

Morgan, Thisba Hutson. "Reminiscences of My Days in the Land of the Ogallala Sioux." *South Dakota Report and Historical Collections* 29 (1958): 21–62.

Northrop, Henry Davenport. *Indian Horrors; or, Massacres by the Red Men.* Philadelphia: National Publishing Co., 1891.

Olson, Louis P. "Mary Clementine Collins, Dacotah Missionary." *North Dakota History* 19 (1952): 59–81.

Peterson, B. J. *The Battle of Wounded Knee.* Gordon, Nebr.: News Publishing Co., 1941.

Piper, Alexander R. "Extracts from Letters Written by Lieutenant Alexander R. Piper . . . during the Sioux Campaign, 1890–1891." In *The Unpublished Papers of the Order of Indian Wars Book Number 10,* edited by John M. Carroll, 11–13. New Brunswick, N.J.: Privately published, 1977.

Powers, William. "The Sioux Omaha Dance." *American Indian Tradition* 8, no. 1 (1961).

Quartermaster General of the Army. *U.S. Army Uniforms and Equipment, 1889*. 1889. Reprint. Lincoln: University of Nebraska Press, 1986.

Seidel, David. *Fremont, Elkhorn & Missouri Valley Railroad Company*. Columbus, Nebr.: Harbor Mist Publications, 1988.

Seymour, Charles G. "The Final Review." *Harper's Weekly*, Feb. 7, 1891.

Sheldon, Addison E. "After Wounded Knee: A Recollection." *Nebraska History* 22, no. 1 (1941): 45.

Sievers, Michael A. "The Historiography of the 'Bloody Field' . . . That Kept the Secret of the Everlasting Word: Wounded Knee." *South Dakota History* 6, no. 1 (1975): 33–54.

Smith, Rex Alan. *Moon of Popping Trees*. 1975. Reprint. Lincoln: University of Nebraska Press, 1975.

Smoak, Gregory E. "The Mormons and the Ghost Dance of 1890." *South Dakota History* 16 (1986): 269–94.

Steele, Matthew Forney. "Buffalo Bill's Bluff." *South Dakota Historical Collections* 9 (1890): 475–85.

Sword, George. "The Story of the Ghost Dance." *Folk-Lorist* (July 1892): 28–36.

Thornton, Russell. *American Indian Holocaust and Survival*. Nor- man: University of Oklahoma Press, 1987.

Utley, Robert M. *Frontier Regulars: The United States Army and the Indian, 1866–1891*. 1973. Reprint. Lincoln: University of Nebraska Press, 1984.

———. *The Indian Frontier of the American West, 1846–1890*. Albuquerque: University of New Mexico Press, 1984.

———. *The Last Days of the Sioux Nation*. New Haven: Yale University Press, 1963.

Viola, Herman J. *Diplomats in Buckskins: A History of Indian Delegations in Washington City*. Washington, D.C.: Smithsonian Institution Press, 1981.

Walker, James R. *Lakota Society*. Edited by Raymond J. DeMallie. Lincoln: University of Nebraska Press, 1982.

Watson, George D., Jr. *Prairie Justice, 1885–1985: A One Hundred Year Study of the Legal System of Chadron and Dawes County*. Chadron, Nebr.: B&B Printing Co., 1986.

Wells, Philip F. "Ninety-six Years among the Indians of the Northwest." *North Dakota History* 15, no. 2 (1948): 85–312.

Wissler, Clark. "Societies and Ceremonial Associations in the Oglala Division of the Teton-Dakota." *Anthropological Papers*, American Museum of Natural History, vol. 11 (1912): 3–99.

Wooster, Robert. *The Military and United States Indian Policy, 1865–1903*. New Haven: Yale University Press, 1988.

Acknowledgments

This book is the result of a collaboration in the finest sense. The three of us worked together and shared research that enhanced our understanding of Wounded Knee. ¶ We in turn benefited from the help of a large number of institutions and individuals, whose contributions were critical to this effort.

INSTITUTIONS

Assumption College Archives, Richardton, North Dakota; Brigham Young University, Harold B. Lee Library, Provo, Utah; Chicago Historical Society; Custer Battlefield National Monument, Crow Agency, Montana; Denver Public Library; Eastern Washington State Historical Society, Spokane; Thomas Gilcrease Institute of American History and Art, Tulsa, Oklahoma; Kansas City, Missouri, Public Library; Kansas State Historical Society, Topeka; Library of Congress; Marquette University, Department of Special Collections and University Archives, Milwaukee, Wisconsin; Minnesota Historical Society, St. Paul; Montana Historical Society, Helena; Museum of the American Indian, New York City; Museum of the Fur Trade, Chadron, Nebraska; National Archives, Washington, D.C., and Kansas City, Missouri Branches; Nebraska Library Commission, Lincoln; New York City Public Library; Newberry Library, Chicago; Ohio Historical Society, Columbus; W. H. Over Museum, Vermillion, South Dakota; Frederic Remington Art Museum, Ogdensburg, New York; Scotts Bluff National Monument, Gering, Nebraska; Smith College, Women's History Archive, Northampton, Massachusetts; Smithsonian Institution, National Anthropological Archives, Washington, D.C.; South Dakota State Historical Society, Robinson Museum, Pierre; Southwest Museum, Los Angeles; State Historical Society of Colorado, Denver; State Historical Society of North Dakota, Bismarck; State Historical Society of Wisconsin, Madison; United States Army Military History Institute, Carlisle Barracks, Pennsylvania; United States Military Academy Library, West Point; University of Colorado Library, Western Historical Collections, Boulder; University of Nebraska–Lincoln, Love Library, and the Center for Great Plains Studies, Collection of Western Art, Lincoln; University of Oklahoma Library, Western History Collections, Norman; University of Wyoming, American Heritage Center, Laramie; and the Wyoming State Archives, Museums and Historical Department, Cheyenne.

INDIVIDUALS

Laurie Baty, Washington, D.C.; John C. Borst, Pierre, South Dakota; Kirk Budd, Rushville, Nebraska; John M. Carroll, Bryan, Texas; Paula R. Fleming, Washington; Mary Dawson Gray and the Henry A. and Francis Williams Dawson Family, Hingham, Massachusetts; Bonnie Gardner, Pierre; Douglas Hartman, Lincoln, Nebraska; James S. Hutchins, Washington; Eddie Little Sky, Kyle, South Dakota; Augie Mastrogiuseppe, Denver, Colorado; Lynn Mitchell, Tucson, Arizona; Reed Miller, Scottsbluff, Nebraska; Eric Paddock, Denver; Don Rickey, Evergreen, Colorado; Pat Rowland, Wounded Knee, South Dakota; Marni Sandwiess, Amherst, Massachusetts; and James Wengert, Omaha, Nebraska. ¶ The authors also wish to thank their colleagues at the Nebraska State Historical Society for their help and advice. Thanks, also, to the American Association for State and Local History, for a 1983 research grant given to John Carter for a study of the photographers who photographed the Plains Indians. That grant supported some of the fundamental research that allowed this book to happen. ¶ Finally, thanks to Eli S. Ricker, who began gathering historical documents, photographs, and interviews with eyewitnesses ninety years ago.

Photograph
Repositories

Plate	Repository	Number
1	National Anthropological Archives, Smithsonian Institution	1659-A
2	National Archives	11-SC.85791
3	Private collection	none
4	Minnesota Historical Society	E93.37 r10
5	Nebraska State Historical Society, Lincoln	I392-163
6	Nebraska State Historical Society, Lincoln	I392-311
7	Library of Congress	USZ62-11567
8	Eastern Washington State Historical Society	F68x
9	Chicago Historical Society	none
10	Eastern Washington State Historical Society	F67x
11	National Anthropological Archives, Smithsonian Institution	55594
12	Nebraska State Historical Society, Lincoln	W938-119-7A
13	Nebraska State Historical Society, Lincoln	W938-119-27B
14	Private collection	none
15	Denver Public Library	F8919 6
16	Denver Public Library	F8917 6
17	Nebraska State Historical Society, Lincoln	T765-9
18	Nebraska State Historical Society, Lincoln	T765-9 (detail)
19	Denver Public Library	F8852 5
20	Nebraska State Historical Society, Lincoln	B191-1
21	Nebraska State Historical Society, Lincoln	I392-181
22	Nebraska State Historical Society, Lincoln	I392-460
23	Museum of the Fur Trade	none
24	Nebraska State Historical Society, Lincoln	I392-450
25	Library of Congress	USZ62-19725
26	Denver Public Library	F8953 5 (left)
		F8962 (right)
27	Nebraska State Historical Society, Lincoln	W938-119-15B

28	Nebraska State Historical Society, Lincoln	I392-58
29	Denver Public Library	F8909
30	Nebraska State Historical Society, Lincoln	W938-119-20A
31	Library of Congress	USZ62-22480
32	Nebraska State Historical Society, Lincoln	W938-119-11B
33	Nebraska State Historical Society, Lincoln	W938-119-21A
34	Nebraska State Historical Society, Lincoln	W938-30 (detail)
35	Kansas State Historical Society	E83.89*14
36	Nebraska State Historical Society, Lincoln	W938-119-16B
37	Nebraska State Historical Society, Lincoln	W938-119-12A
38	Nebraska State Historical Society, Lincoln	W938-119-48D
39	Kansas State Historical Society	E99.S6 D9 *1
40	Library of Congress	15017
41	Kansas State Historical Society	E99.S6 I JRC *1
42	Nebraska State Historical Society, Lincoln	T765-18
43	Nebraska State Historical Society, Lincoln	W938-30
44	Nebraska State Historical Society, Lincoln	I392-250
45	Nebraska State Historical Society, Lincoln	W938-119-42B
46	Nebraska State Historical Society, Lincoln	W938-119-36A
47	Nebraska State Historical Society, Lincoln	W938-119-40B
48	Nebraska State Historical Society, Lincoln	W938-119-19A
49	Private collection	none
50	Nebraska State Historical Society, Lincoln	W938-63
51	Nebraska State Historical Society, Lincoln	W938-61
52	Nebraska State Historical Society, Lincoln	T765-21
53	Nebraska State Historical Society, Lincoln	W938-5
54	Nebraska State Historical Society, Lincoln	T765-29
55	Nebraska State Historical Society, Lincoln	W938-119-13B

56	Nebraska State Historical Society, Lincoln	I392-37
57	Private collection	none
58	Nebraska State Historical Society, Lincoln	W938-119-45B
59	Nebraska State Historical Society, Lincoln	I392-403A
60	Minnesota Historical Society	E93.4r1
61	State Historical Society of North Dakota	A-1947
62	Library of Congress	USZ62-17591
63	Nebraska State Historical Society, Lincoln	W938-66
64	Nebraska State Historical Society, Lincoln	W938-119-19B
65	Nebraska State Historical Society, Lincoln	W938-102
66	Nebraska State Historical Society, Lincoln	W938-65
67	Kansas City Public Library	none
68	Huntington Library	none
69	Nebraska State Historical Society, Lincoln	W938-64/44A
70	Nebraska State Historical Society, Lincoln	W938-44
71	Custer Battlefield National Monument	723
72	Nebraska State Historical Society, Lincoln	W938-43
73	National Anthropological Archives, Smithsonian Institution	3200-B-2
74	National Anthropological Archives, Smithsonian Institution	5501842
75	Nebraska State Historical Society, Lincoln	W938-119-17B
76	Nebraska State Historical Society, Lincoln	W938-45
77	Nebraska State Historical Society, Lincoln	W938-46
78	Nebraska State Historical Society, Lincoln	W938-47
79	Nebraska State Historical Society, Lincoln	T765-32
80	Library of Congress	LCZ62-27931
81	Denver Public Library	F89385
82	Denver Public Library	F88435
83	Nebraska State Historical Society, Lincoln	W938-119-13A

84	University of Wyoming, American Heritage Center	In2-bat-wk
85	South Dakota State Historical Society	none
86	Library of Congress	USZ62-11970
87	Nebraska State Historical Society, Lincoln	W938-119-3A
88	Huntington Library	Album 178 #14
89	South Dakota State Historical Society	none
90	Nebraska State Historical Society, Lincoln	R539-104
91	Library of Congress	USZ62-22971
92	Nebraska State Historical Society, Lincoln	I392-186
93	Denver Public Library	F32086
94	Denver Public Library	F88213
95	Denver Public Library	F89505
96	Nebraska State Historical Society, Lincoln	W938-32
97	Nebraska State Historical Society, Lincoln	R659-2599
98	Nebraska State Historical Society, Lincoln	W938-17
99	Nebraska State Historical Society, Lincoln	I392-239
100	Nebraska State Historical Society, Lincoln	W938-119-39B
101	South Dakota State Historical Society	none
102	Nebraska State Historical Society, Lincoln	W938-119-12B
103	Nebraska State Historical Society, Lincoln	W938-119-4B
104	Nebraska State Historical Society, Lincoln	W938-119-50B
105	Nebraska State Historical Society, Lincoln	I392-242
106	Nebraska State Historical Society, Lincoln	W938-7
107	Nebraska State Historical Society, Lincoln	T765-4
108	Denver Public Library	F89485
109	Nebraska State Historical Society, Lincoln	W938-119-30B
110	Nebraska State Historical Society, Lincoln	W938-119-10B
111	Montana Historical Society	954-832

112	Eastern Washington State Historical Society	F65x
113	Library of Congress	USZ62-11570
114	Nebraska State Historical Society, Lincoln	W938-70
115	Nebraska State Historical Society, Lincoln	I392-173
116	Nebraska State Historical Society, Lincoln	I392-173A
117	Nebraska State Historical Society, Lincoln	W938-119-47B
118	South Dakota State Historical Society	none
119	Nebraska State Historical Society, Lincoln	T765-12
120	Nebraska State Historical Society, Lincoln	W938-119-44A
121	Library of Congress	USZ62-50458
122	South Dakota State Historical Society	none
123	Library of Congress	USZ62-78529
124	Nebraska State Historical Society, Lincoln	W938-119-37A
125	Nebraska State Historical Society, Lincoln	W938-119-9A
126	State Historical Society of Colorado	3536 E816 D7
127	Nebraska State Historical Society, Lincoln	I392-266x
128	Nebraska State Historical Society, Lincoln	I392-265x
129	Nebraska State Historical Society, Lincoln	W938-119-20B
130	Nebraska State Historical Society, Lincoln	W938-119-5B
131	Denver Public Library	F8808
132	Nebraska State Historical Society, Lincoln	W938-119-8A
133	Denver Public Library	none
134	National Anthropological Archives, Smithsonian Institution	SPC005522.00
135	Nebraska State Historical Society, Lincoln	W938-119-38A
136	Denver Public Library	none
137	Nebraska State Historical Society, Lincoln	W938-59A
138	Nebraska State Historical Society, Lincoln	W938-49
139	Nebraska State Historical Society, Lincoln	I392-243

Index

Other volumes in the Great Plains Photography Series include **Dreams in Dry Places** by Roger Bruhn, and **A Harmony of the Arts: The Nebraska State Capitol**, edited by Frederick C. Luebke

This book was designed and typeset,
using the Joanna types of Eric Gill,
at the University of Nebraska Press
in its 50th year of publishing ❧